Praxis 0411

Educational Leadership: Administration and Supervision

Teacher Certification Exam

By: Sharon Wynne, M.S.

XAMonline, INC.
Boston

To obtain permission(s) to use the material from this work for any purpose including workshops or seminars, please submit a written request to:

XAMonline, Inc.
25 First Street, Suite 106
Cambridge, MA 02141
Toll Free 1-800-509-4128
Email: info@xamonline.com
Web: www.xamonline.com
Fax: 1-617-583-5552

Library of Congress Cataloging-in-Publication Data

Wynne, Sharon A.
　　Educational Leadership: Administration and Supervision 0411: Teacher Certification / Sharon A. Wynne. – 4th ed. ISBN 978-1-60787-329-7
　　　1. Educational Leadership 0411.　　　2. Study Guides.　　　3. Praxis
　　　4. Teachers' Certification & Licensure.　　5. Careers

Disclaimer:
The opinions expressed in this publication are the sole works of XAMonline and were created independently from the National Education Association,
Educational Testing Service, or any State Department of Education, National Evaluation Systems or other testing affiliates.

Between the time of publication and printing, state specific standards as well as testing formats and website information may change that is not included in part or in whole within this product. Sample test questions are developed by XAMonline and reflect similar content as on real tests; however, they are not former tests. XAMonline assembles content that aligns with state standards but makes no claims nor guarantees teacher candidates a passing score. Numerical scores are determined by testing companies such as NES or ETS and then are compared with individual state standards. A passing score varies from state to state.

Printed in the United States of America　　　　　　　　　　œ-1

PRAXIS: Educational Leadership: Administration and Supervision 0411
ISBN: 978-1-60787-329-7

Section 1 About XAMonline

XAMonline – A Specialty Teacher Certification Company

Created in 1996, XAMonline was the first company to publish study guides for state-specific teacher certification examinations. Founder Sharon Wynne found it frustrating that materials were not available for teacher certification preparation and decided to create the first single, state-specific guide. XAMonline has grown into a company of over 1800 contributors and writers and offers over 300 titles for the entire PRAXIS series and every state examination. No matter what state you plan on teaching in, XAMonline has a unique teacher certification study guide just for you.

XAMonline – Value and Innovation

We are committed to providing value and innovation. Our print-on-demand technology allows us to be the first in the market to reflect changes in test standards and user feedback as they occur. Our guides are written by experienced teachers who are experts in their fields. And, our content reflects the highest standards of quality. Comprehensive practice tests with varied levels of rigor means that your study experience will closely match the actual in-test experience.

To date, XAMonline has helped nearly 600,000 teachers pass their certification or licensing exams. Our commitment to preparation exceeds simply providing the proper material for study – it extends to helping teachers **gain mastery** of the subject matter, giving them the **tools** to become the most effective classroom leaders possible, and ushering today's students toward a **successful future**.

Section 2 About this Study Guide

Purpose of this Guide
Is there a little voice inside of you saying, "Am I ready?" Our goal is to replace that little voice and remove all doubt with a new voice that says, "I AM READY. **Bring it on!**" by offering the highest quality of teacher certification study guides.

Organization of Content
You will see that while every test may start with overlapping general topics, each are very unique in the skills they wish to test. Only XAMonline presents custom content that analyzes deeper than a title, a subarea, or an objective. Only XAMonline presents content and sample test assessments along with **focus statements**, the deepest-level rationale and interpretation of the skills that are unique to the exam.

Title and field number of test
→Each exam has its own name and number. XAMonline's guides are written to give you the content you need to know for the specific exam you are taking. You can be confident when you buy our guide that it contains the information you need to study for the specific test you are taking.

Subareas
→These are the major content categories found on the exam. XAMonline's guides are written to cover all of the subareas found in the test frameworks developed for the exam.

Objectives
→These are standards that are unique to the exam and represent the main subcategories of the subareas/content categories. XAMonline's guides are written to address every specific objective required to pass the exam.

Focus statements
→These are examples and interpretations of the objectives. You find them in parenthesis directly following the objective. They provide detailed examples of the range, type, and level of content that appear on the test questions. **Only XAMonline's guides drill down to this level.**

How do We Compare with Our Competitors?
XAMonline – drills down to the focus statement level
CliffsNotes and REA – organized at the objective level
Kaplan – provides only links to content
MoMedia – content not specific to the test

Each subarea is divided into manageable sections that cover the specific skill areas. Explanations are easy-to-understand and thorough. You'll find that every test answer contains a rejoinder so if you need a refresher or further review after taking the test, you'll know exactly to which section you must return.

How to Use this Book

Our informal polls show that most people begin studying up to 8 weeks prior to the test date, so start early. Then ask yourself some questions: How much do you really know? Are you coming to the test straight from your teacher-education program or are you having to review subjects you haven't considered in 10 years? Either way, take a **diagnostic or assessment test** first. Also, spend time on sample tests so that you become accustomed to the way the actual test will appear.

This guide comes with an online diagnostic test of 30 questions found online at www.XAMonline.com. It is a little boot camp to get you up for the task and reveal things about your compendium of knowledge in general. Although this guide is structured to follow the order of the test, you are not required to study in that order. By finding a time-management and study plan that fits your life you will be more effective. The results of your diagnostic or self-assessment test can be a guide for how to manage your time and point you towards an area that needs more attention.

Week	Activity
8 weeks prior to test	Take a diagnostic test found at www.XAMonline.com
7 weeks prior to test	Review the competencies and skills in each chapter to see which sections you feel strong in and which sections you feel you need to focus on.
6-3 weeks prior to test	For each of these weeks, choose a content area to study. You don't have to go in the order of the book. It may be that you start with the content that needs the most review. Alternately, you may want to ease yourself into plan by starting with the most familiar material.
2 weeks prior to test	Take the sample test, score it, and create a review plan for the final week before the test.
1 week prior to test	Following your plan (which will likely be aligned with the areas that need the most review) go back and study the sections that align with the questions you may have gotten wrong. Then go back and study the sections related to the questions you answered correctly. If need be, create flashcards and drill yourself on any area that you makes you anxious.

Section 3 About the PRAXIS Exams

What is PRAXIS?
PRAXIS II tests measure the knowledge of specific content areas in K-12 education. The test is a way of insuring that educators are prepared to not only teach in a particular subject area, but also have the necessary teaching skills to be effective. The Educational Testing Service administers the test in most states and has worked with the states to develop the material so that it is appropriate for state standards.

PRAXIS Points
1. The PRAXIS Series comprises more than 140 different tests in over 70 different subject areas.
2. Over 90% of the PRAXIS tests measure subject area knowledge.
3. The purpose of the test is to measure whether the teacher candidate possesses a sufficient level of knowledge and skills to perform job duties effectively and responsibly.
4. Your state sets the acceptable passing score.
5. Any candidate, whether from a traditional teaching-preparation path or an alternative route, can seek to enter the teaching profession by taking a PRAXIS test.
6. PRAXIS tests are updated regularly to ensure current content.

Often **your own state's requirements** determine whether or not you should take any particular test. The most reliable source of information regarding this is either your state's Department of Education or the Educational Testing Service. Either resource should also have a complete list of testing centers and dates. Test dates vary by subject area and not all test dates necessarily include your particular test, so be sure to check carefully.

If you are in a teacher-education program, check with the Education Department or the Certification Officer for specific information for testing and testing timelines. The Certification Office should have most of the information you need.

If you choose an alternative route to certification you can either rely on our website at www.XAMonline.com or on the resources provided by an alternative certification program. Many states now have specific agencies devoted to alternative certification and there are some national organizations as well:
- National Center for Education Information
  http://www.ncei.com/Alt-Teacher-Cert.htm
- National Associate for Alternative Certification
  http://www.alt-teachercert.org/index.asp

Interpreting Test Results

Contrary to what you may have heard, the results of a PRAXIS test are not based on time. More accurately, you will be scored on the raw number of points you earn in relation to the raw number of points available. Each question is worth one raw point. It is likely to your benefit to complete as many questions in the time allotted, but it will not necessarily work to your advantage if you hurry through the test.

Follow the guidelines provided by ETS for interpreting your score. The web site offers a sample test score sheet and clearly explains how the scores are scaled and what to expect if you have an essay portion on your test.

Scores are usually available by phone within a month of the test date and scores will be sent to your chosen institution(s) within six weeks. Additionally, ETS now makes online, downloadable reports available for 45 days from the reporting date.

It is **critical** that you be aware of your own state's passing score. Your raw score may qualify you to teach in some states, but not all. ETS administers the test and assigns a score, but the states make their own interpretations and, in some cases, consider combined scores if you are testing in more than one area.

What's on the Test?

PRAXIS tests vary from subject to subject and sometimes even within subject area. For PRAXIS Educational Leadership: Administration and Supervision (041), the test lasts for 2 hours and consists of approximately 95 multiple-choice questions. The breakdown of the questions is as follows:

Category	Approximate Number of Questions	Approximate Percentage of the test
I: Vision and Goals	18	19%
II: Teaching and Learning	24	25%
III: Managing Organizational Systems & Safety	13	14%
IV: Collaborating with Key Stakeholders	12	13%
V: Ethics and Integrity	16	17%
VI: The Education System	12	12%

Question Types

You're probably thinking, enough already, I want to study! Indulge us a little longer while we explain that there is actually more than one type of multiple-choice question. You can thank us later after you realize how well prepared you are for your exam.

1. **Complete the Statement.** The name says it all. In this question type you'll be asked to choose the correct completion of a given statement. For example: The Dolch Basic Sight Words consist of a relatively short list of words that children should be able to:
   a. Sound out
   b. Know the meaning of
   c. Recognize on sight
   d. Use in a sentence

   The correct answer is C. In order to check your answer, test out the statement by adding the choices to the end of it.

2. **Which of the Following.** One way to test your answer choice for this type of question is to replace the phrase "which of the following" with your selection. Use this example: Which of the following words is one of the twelve most frequently used in children's reading texts:
   a. There
   b. This
   c. The
   d. An

   Don't look! Test your answer. _____ is one of the twelve most frequently used in children's reading texts. Did you guess C? Then you guessed correctly.

3. **Roman Numeral Choices.** This question type is used when there is more than one possible correct answer. For example: Which of the following two arguments accurately supports the use of cooperative learning as an effective method of instruction?
   I. Cooperative learning groups facilitate healthy competition between individuals in the group.
   II. Cooperative learning groups allow academic achievers to carry or cover for academic underachievers.
   III. Cooperative learning groups make each student in the group accountable for the success of the group.
   IV. Cooperative learning groups make it possible for students to reward other group members for achieving.
   > A. I and II
   > B. II and III
   > C. I and III
   > D. III and IV

   Notice that the question states there are **two** possible answers. It's best to read all the possibilities first before looking at the answer choices. In this case, the correct answer is D.

4. **Negative Questions.** This type of question contains words such as "not," "least," and "except." Each correct answer will be the statement that does **not** fit the situation described in the question. Such as: Multicultural education is **not**
   a. An idea or concept
   b. A "tack-on" to the school curriculum
   c. An educational reform movement
   d. A process

Think to yourself that the statement could be anything but the correct answer. This question form is more open to interpretation than other types, so read carefully and don't forget that you're answering a negative statement.

5. **Questions That Include Graphs, Tables, or Reading Passages.** As ever, read the question carefully. It likely asks for a very specific answer and not broad interpretation of the visual. Here is a simple (though not statistically accurate) example of a graph question: In the following graph in how many years did more men take the NYSTCE exam than women?

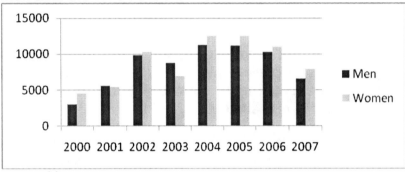

   a. None
   b. One
   c. Two
   d. Three

It may help you to simply circle the two years that answer the question. Make sure you've read the question thoroughly and once you've made your determination, double check your work. The correct answer is C.

Section 4 Helpful Hints

Study Tips

1. **You are what you eat.** Certain foods aid the learning process by releasing natural memory enhancers called CCKs (cholecystokinin) composed of tryptophan, choline, and phenylalanine. All of these chemicals enhance the neurotransmitters associated with memory and certain foods release memory enhancing chemicals. A light meal or snacks from the following foods fall into this category:

    - Milk
    - Nuts and seeds
    - Rice
    - Oats
    - Eggs
    - Turkey
    - Fish

    The better the connections, the more you comprehend!

2. **See the forest for the trees.** In other words, get the concept before you look at the details. One way to do this is to take notes as you read, paraphrasing or summarizing in your own words. Putting the concept in terms that are comfortable and familiar may increase retention.

3. **Question authority.** Ask why, why, why. Pull apart written material paragraph by paragraph and don't forget the captions under the illustrations. For example, if a heading reads *Stream Erosion* put it in the form of a question (why do streams erode? Or what is stream erosion?) then find the answer within the material. If you train your mind to think in this manner you will learn more and prepare yourself for answering test questions.

4. **Play mind games**. Using your brain for reading or puzzles keeps it flexible. Even with a limited amount of time your brain can take in data (much like a computer) and store it for later use. In ten minutes you can: read two paragraphs (at least), quiz yourself with flash cards, or review notes. Even if you don't fully understand something on the first pass, your mind stores it for recall, which is why frequent reading or review increases chances of retention and comprehension.

5. **The pen is mightier than the sword.** Learn to take great notes. A by-product of our modern culture is that we have grown accustomed to getting our information in short doses. We've subconsciously trained ourselves to assimilate information into neat little packages. Messy notes fragment the flow of information. Your notes can be much clearer with proper formatting. *The Cornell Method* is one such format. This method was popularized in *How to Study in College,* Ninth Edition, by Walter Pauk. You can benefit from the method without purchasing an additional book by simply looking the method up online. Below is a sample of how *The Cornell Method* can be adapted for use with this guide.

← 2 ½" →	← 6" →
Cue Column	**Note Taking Column**
	1. **Record:** During your reading, use the note-taking column to record important points.
	2. **Questions:** As soon as you finish a section, formulate questions based on the notes in the right-hand column. Writing questions helps to clarify meanings, reveal relationships, establish community, and strengthen memory. Also, the writing of questions sets the state for exam study later.
	3. **Recite:** Cover the note-taking column with a sheet of paper. Then, looking at the questions or cue-words in the question and cue column only, say aloud, in your own words, the answers to the questions, facts, or ideas indicated by the cue words.
	4. **Reflect:** Reflect on the material by asking yourself questions.
	5. **Review:** Spend at least ten minutes every week reviewing all your previous notes. Doing so helps you retain ideas and topics for the exam.
↑ 2" ↓	**Summary**
	After reading, use this space to summarize the notes from each page.

*Adapted from *How to Study in College,* Ninth Edition, by Walter Pauk, ©2008 Wadsworth

6. **Place yourself in exile and set the mood.** Set aside a particular place and time to study that best suits your personal needs and biorhythms. If you're a night person, burn the midnight oil. If you're a morning person set yourself up with some coffee and get to it. Make your study time and place as free from distraction as possible and surround yourself with what you need, be it silence or music. Studies have shown that music can aid in concentration, absorption, and retrieval of information. Not all music, though. Classical music is said to work best.

7. **Get pointed in the right direction.** Use arrows to point to important passages or pieces of information. It's easier to read than a page full of yellow highlights. Highlighting can be used sparingly, but add an arrow to the margin to call attention to it.

8. **Check your budget.** You should at least review all the content material before your test, but allocate the most amount of time to the areas that need the most refreshing. It sounds obvious, but it's easy to forget. You can use the study rubric above to balance your study budget.

> The proctor will write the start time where it can be seen and then, later, provide the time remaining, typically 15 minutes before the end of the test.

Testing Tips

1. **Get smart, play dumb.** Sometimes a question is just a question. No one is out to trick you, so don't assume that the test writer is looking for something other than what was asked. Stick to the question as written and don't overanalyze.

2. **Do a double take.** Read test questions and answer choices at least twice because it's easy to miss something, to transpose a word or some letters. If you have no idea what the correct answer is, skip it and come back later if there's time. If you're still clueless, it's okay to guess. Remember, you're scored on the number of questions you answer correctly and you're not penalized for wrong answers. The worst case scenario is that you miss a point from a good guess.

3. **Turn it on its ear.** The syntax of a question can often provide a clue, so make things interesting and turn the question into a statement to see if it changes the meaning or relates better (or worse) to the answer choices.

4. **Get out your magnifying glass.** Look for hidden clues in the questions because it's difficult to write a multiple-choice question without giving away part of the answer in the options presented. In most questions you can readily eliminate one or two potential answers, increasing your chances of answering correctly to 50/50, which will help out if you've skipped a question and gone back to it (see tip #2).

5. **Call it intuition.** Often your first instinct is correct. If you've been studying the content you've likely absorbed something and have subconsciously retained the knowledge. On questions you're not sure about trust your instincts because a first impression is usually correct.

6. **Graffiti.** Sometimes it's a good idea to mark your answers directly on the test booklet and go back to fill in the optical scan sheet later. You don't get extra points for perfectly blackened ovals. If you choose to manage your test this way, be sure not to mismark your answers when you transcribe to the scan sheet.

7. **Become a clock-watcher.** You have a set amount of time to answer the questions. Don't get bogged down laboring over a question you're not sure about when there are ten others you could answer more readily. If you choose to follow the advice of tip #6, be sure you leave time near the end to go back and fill in the scan sheet.

Do the Drill

No matter how prepared you feel it's sometimes a good idea to apply Murphy's Law. So the following tips might seem silly, mundane, or obvious, but we're including them anyway.

1. **Remember, you are what you eat, so bring a snack.** Choose from the list of energizing foods that appear earlier in the introduction.

2. **You're not too sexy for your test.** Wear comfortable clothes. You'll be distracted if your belt is too tight, or if you're too cold or too hot.

3. **Lie to yourself.** Even if you think you're a prompt person, pretend you're not and leave plenty of time to get to the testing center. Map it out ahead of time and do a dry run if you have to. There's no need to add road rage to your list of anxieties.

4. **Bring sharp, number 2 pencils.** It may seem impossible to forget this need from your school days, but you might. And make sure the erasers are intact, too.

5. **No ticket, no test.** Bring your admission ticket as well as **two** forms of identification, including one with a picture and signature. You will not be admitted to the test without these things.

6. **You can't take it with you.** Leave any study aids, dictionaries, notebooks, computers and the like at home. Certain tests **do** allow a scientific or four-function calculator, so check ahead of time if your test does.

7. **Prepare for the desert.** Any time spent on a bathroom break **cannot** be made up later, so use your judgment on the amount you eat or drink.

8. **Quiet, Please!** Keeping your own time is a good idea, but not with a timepiece that has a loud ticker. If you use a watch, take it off and place it nearby but not so that it distracts you. And **silence your cell phone.**

To the best of our ability, we have compiled the content you need to know in this book and in the accompanying online resources. The rest is up to you. You can use the study and testing tips or you can follow your own methods. Either way, you can be confident that there aren't any missing pieces of information and there shouldn't be any surprises in the content on the test.

If you have questions about test fees, registration, electronic testing, or other content verification issues please visit www.ets.org.

Good luck!
Sharon Wynne
Founder, XAMonline

Table of Contents

DOMAIN I VISION AND GOALS

COMPETENCY 001   VISION AND GOALS FOR TEACHING AND LEARNING

Skill 1.1   Analyzes multiple sources of information and data about current practice prior to developing/revising a vision and goals

Education involves an inseparable interaction between teaching and learning. Schools are expected to produce children who are well educated and who enjoy being life-long learners. Bryson (2011)[1] explains that educational systems are also expected to help communities and firms compete more effectively. Thus, education is seen as an economic and industrial engine producing individuals who are prepared to contribute to society. Schools must have strategic plans with visions and goals that are in line with mandates set at the national, state, and local levels.

To create a strong strategic plan that will face the least resistance. Current, effective practices should be incorporated and data and information should be gathered and analyzed. Then, administrators can determine where the school or system is strong and where it needs to change.

1.1 A   Selects the appropriate school goal based on data

To select appropriate school goals, the principal must gather as much information as possible from stakeholders in the school and in the wider community. The information gathering process must be systematic and address issues such as the most reliable information source(s), additional data sources, plan for data analysis, whom to involve and when, and what to do with the information obtained from this process.

This is an evidence-based approach to planning. It relies on data to define the areas where the school is strong and the areas where specific goals are needed to guide improvement efforts. As a social system, schools have many areas that impact upon and are impacted by each other. Academics cannot be the only area where administrators place their focus. However, school goals primarily deal with academics and the process for selecting these goals can be followed for other areas such as safety, maintenance, citizenship, and school culture.

Academic planning typically begins with a review of assessment data. Each subject area has pre- and post- assessments that are used to evaluate the skill level and ability of each learner. Assessments identify areas where teachers can construct meaningful lessons that are accessible to all learners. To reap the full benefits of assessment tools and strategies quantitative data must track student learning in various subjects. It is the job of the administrator to ensure that assessments are congruent with academic content areas.

---

[1] Bryson, J.M. (2011). Strategic planning for public and nonprofit organizations: A guide to strengthening and sustaining organizational achievement.

These data measure student growth during the school year and from year to year, rather than measuring student achievement at a single point in time. Implementing an ongoing tracking system ensures that teachers and administrators can understand and influence growth for all students, regardless of achievement status, age, or class groupings. Analyzing these growth measures over time will also help to determine how student achievement is aligned with district or state standards. After looking at the short and long term data, the administrator can determine the most pressing challenges. Specific goals would then be selected to guide improvement efforts in the identified areas.

<u>1.1 B</u>   Analyzes data to write a school goal or determines if vision and goals are appropriate

In most instances, successful goal attainment requires a team approach. Therefore, the entire staff should be involved from the very beginning; build consensus and support at the stage of analyzing the data. While there is no single, best source of data, in the age of accountability and testing, districts or states have mandatory assessments. It is most efficient to utilize these data in determining the vision and goals for the school. A principal or superintendent may also choose to analyze data on national assessments such as the ACT or SAT. It can also be helpful to review results from teacher-created tests, particularly if they provide qualitative data to enhance the quantitative numbers that are provided by standardized tests.

To select the best source of data, a school leader must understand several basic assessment-related concepts. First, data must be accurate. Accuracy is determined by the usability of the instrument and the consistency of measurement, which is observed through reliability and validity of the instruments.

Validity is the extent to which a test measures what it is intended to measure. For example, a test may lack validity if it was designed to measure creative writing but it is also used to measure handwriting.

Reliability refers to the consistency of the test to measure what it should measure. For example, the items on a true-or-false quiz, given by a classroom teacher, are reliable if they convey the same meaning every time the quiz is administered to similar groups of students under similar conditions. In other words, there is no ambiguity or confusion with the items on the quiz.

The difference between validity and reliability can be visualized in terms of throwing darts at a dartboard. There is validity if the dart hits the target (an assessment measures what it is intended to measure); it is reliable if the same spot is hit time after time (the assessment consistently measures what it should measure). The goal should be to develop assessments that are both valid and reliable (every time the assessment is administered, it measures what it is intended to measure).

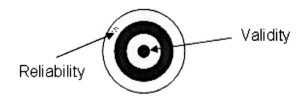

Reliability — Validity

Usability, another factor in the evaluation process, refers to practical considerations such as scoring procedures, level of difficulty, and time to administer the test. The usability of a test is questionable, for example, if the scoring procedures had to be changed to accommodate local financial circumstances or if the allotted time for a test had to be reduced because of other circumstances.

STANDARDIZED ACHIEVEMENT TESTS

Because the purpose of assessment instruments is data gathering, it is important to use various forms of information-gathering tools to assess the knowledge and progress of students. Standardized achievement tests have become a central tool in education today, particularly due to No Child Left Behind. The widespread use of standardized achievement tests to provide information for accountability to the public has driven many teachers to "teach to the test" and embrace more objective formats of teaching and learning. These tests are very limited in what they measure and too often they are used to make major decisions for which they are not designed.

Standardized achievement tests can be norm-referenced or criterion-referenced. In norm-referenced measurements the performance of the student is compared with the performance of other students who also took the same test. The original group of students who took the test establishes the norm. Norms can be based on age, sex, grade level, geographical location, ethnicity, or other broad classifications.

Norm-Referenced Achievement Tests
Standardized, norm-referenced achievement tests are designed to measure what a student knows in a particular subject in relation to other students with similar characteristics. The test batteries provide a broad scope of content area coverage so that the test can be used on a large scale in many different states and school districts. However, the questions may not measure the goals and content emphasized in a particular local curriculum. Therefore, using standardized tests to assess the success of the curriculum or teachers' effectiveness should be avoided (McMillan, 1997).

Norm-referenced standardized achievement tests produce different types of scores that are useful in different ways. The most common types of scores are the percentile ranks, or percentile scores, grade-equivalent scores, stanines, and percentage of items answered correctly.

The percentile score indicates how a student's performance compares to the norming group. It indicates what percentage of the norming group was outscored by a particular student taking the test. For example, a student scoring in the eightieth percentile did better than 80 percent of the students in the norming group. Or, 20 percent of the norming group scored above the particular student and 80 percent scored below. The scores are indicative of relative strengths and weaknesses. A student may show consistent strengths in language arts and consistent weakness in mathematics. Yet one could not base remediation solely on these conclusions without a closer item analysis or a closer review of the objectives measured by the test.

The grade-equivalency score is expressed by year and month in school for each student. It is used to measure growth and progress. It indicates where a student stands in reference to the norming group. For example, a second-grade student who obtained a grade-equivalent score of 4.5 on the language arts section of the test is really not achieving at the fourth-grade, five-month level, as one might think. The 4.5 grade equivalence means that the second grader has achieved at about the same level as a student of the norming group who is in the fifth month of the fourth grade. However, when compared to other second graders in the norming group, the student may be about average.

A point of consideration with grade equivalence is that one may never know how well the second grader might do if placed in the fourth grade or how poorly the second grader might do if given the fourth-grade test compared to other second graders in the norming group.

Stanines are nine-point scales used for normalized test scores, with 1-3 below average, 4-6 average, and 7-9 above average. The word is a combination of "standard" and "nine." A stanine indicates where the score is located on the normal curve for the norming group. Stanines are statistically determined but are not as precise as percentile ranking because they only give the area in which the score is located, but not the precise location. Using stanines to report standard scores is still found to be practical and easy to understand for many parents and school personnel.

Finally, achievement test scores can be reported by percentage of items answered correctly. This form of reporting may not be very meaningful when there are only a few questions or items in a particular category. This makes it difficult to determine whether the student guessed well at the items, was just lucky at selecting the right answers, or knowingly chose the correct responses.

Criterion-Referenced Achievement Tests
Criterion-referenced standardized achievement tests are designed to measure the student's performance that is directly related to specific educational objectives, thus indicating what the student can or cannot do. For example, the test may measure how well a student can subtract by regrouping in the tens place or how well a student can identify the long vowel sound in specific words.

Criterion-referenced tests are specific to a particular curriculum, which allows the determination of the effectiveness of the curriculum, as well as specific skills acquired by the students. They also provide information needed to plan for future student needs. Because of the recognized value of criterion-referenced standardized achievement tests, many publishers have developed tailor-made tests to correlate with state and districts' general goals and specific learning objectives by pulling from a test bank of field-tested items. The test scores are reported by percentage of items answered correctly to indicate mastery or non-mastery.

APTITUDE TESTS

Aptitude tests are another standardized form of testing that measure the cognitive abilities of students. They also measure potential and capacity for learning. While they do not test specific academic ability, the student's ability level is influenced by his or her experiences in and out of the academic setting. Aptitude tests are used to predict achievement and for advanced placement of students.

OTHER FORMS OF ASSESSMENT

Teacher-made tests are also evaluative instruments designed by classroom teachers to measure the attainment of objectives. While they may lack validity, they serve the immediate purpose of measuring instructional outcomes. Teacher-made tests should be constructed to measure specific objectives, but they also take into account the nature of the behavior that is being measured. Among teacher-made tests are multiple choice, essay, quizzes, matching, alternative choices (yes/no, agree/disagree, etc.), and completion items (fill-in-the-blanks).

Portfolio assessment is fast becoming a leading form of assessment, in which the student and teacher collect sample work in a systematic and organized manner to provide evidence of accomplishments and progress toward attaining specific objectives.

Certainly, testing is very important in the assessment of students' progress, but there are other sources of information that can be used for assessment as well. For example, conferencing and cumulative records of a child's work may also provide factual information for cognitive and psychomotor assessments. Other information sources may include interviews, diaries, self-assessments, observations, and simulations.

Skill 1.2	**Implements a vision and goals with high, measurable expectations for all students and educators**

Roland Barth wrote that "a school's culture has far more influence on life and learning in the schoolhouse than the president of the country, the state department of education, the superintendent, the school board, or even the principal, teachers, and parents can ever have."

Principals, as instructional leaders, are charged with the seemingly mutually opposed challenges of "leaving no child behind" and "racing to the top." Meeting these goals involves instituting fundamental changes in school culture. It is no longer acceptable for the majority of students to do well. Educators are now required to ensure high levels of learning for all students. Today's school leaders must lead the staff and community in efforts to close the achievement gap between high and low performers, develop students' thinking and problem-solving skills, and attend to students' social and emotional development.

School leaders must articulate and implement an agreed vision of learning, and ensure that it is shared by the school community. Leadership to create a campus culture of high expectations requires a sense of urgency and a mix of pressure and support. If a principal is assigned to lead a school where many students are struggling, there is a need to fast track the change by pushing hard on standards, providing quality support material and examples of successful practice, and providing focused professional development. As student achievement increases, the principal should shift to capacity building to encourage local ownership. Leaders should strive to move from tighter to looser control and from external control to internal commitment.

Michael Fullan has written about the culture of "dependency" among schools—the tendency to wait for solutions from outside. Any kind of improvement is a function of learning to do the right thing in the setting where you work. Ultimately no amount of outside motivation can specify the best solutions for a particular situation. Principals who help their schools to form Professional Learning Communities (PLCs) embrace the notion that the primary purpose of a school is learning, not just teaching. Educators in PLCs examine the practices of their schools to find ways to ensure that all children will learn.

Professional Learning Communities:

- Continuously examine what is worthwhile and how to get there.
- Work together to figure out what is needed to achieve the goal of "no child left behind".
- Understand that internal commitment and ingenuity does not come from outside the school; expertise lies within.
- Understand that change is forever. Problems don't stay solved, so you have to keep learning to do the right thing over and over again.

"Schools that establish high expectations for all students . . . and provide the support necessary to achieve these expectations . . . have high rates of academic success (Brook et al., 1989; Edmonds, 1986; Howard, 1990; Levin, 1988; Rutter et al., 1979; Slavin et al., 1989). Schools with high expectations and incisive, adequate support are successful schools that share certain characteristics: an emphasis on academics, clear expectations and regulations, high levels of student participation, and alternative resources such as library facilities, vocational work opportunities, art, music, and extracurricular activities.

Conveying positive and high expectations to students occurs in several ways. One of the most obvious and powerful is through personal relationships in which teachers and other school staff communicate to students, "This work is important; I know you can do it; I won't give up on you" (Howard, 1990). Successful teachers look for children's strengths and interests, and use these as starting points for learning. A relationship that conveys high expectations to students can internalize these beliefs in students and develop self-esteem and self-efficacy.

1.2 A   Develops a plan for implementing vision and goals

When implementing the selected vision and goals, the school leader must make sure they are aligned with state and federal requirements. The content must be accessible, rigorous, and relevant for student success. Principals must then provide direction to school staff on how to more effectively meet the state standards and federal mandates for student learning. Guidance can be provided through professional development sessions or in brief but specific training during staff meetings. To facilitate teacher sessions, administrators must engage in professional opportunities themselves. Principals should research current state standards and identify evidence-based practices that can be adopted at their schools.

When the goal is academically-focused, it will require adjustments to the curriculum and should include pre- and post-tests to measure knowledge growth. Teachers should also use performance-based assessments to ascertain students' ability to apply the subject-area content. By developing their knowledge of each grade level's standards, administrators can empower teachers and communicate high expectations for classroom instruction. Teachers then create challenging lessons, incorporate a variety of learning styles, administer outcome-based assessments, and use feedback to determine instructional effectiveness and levels of student learning.

1.2 B   Determines if expectations are measureable, rigorous, and connected to vision and goals

Each member of the learning community will have expectations of what teachers and students should know and be able to do. The administrator will need to help stakeholders identify, prioritize, and make decisions about these expectations. Schools do not exist in a vacuum; they are open systems, interrelated with the environments within which they exist. The external environment of schools includes parents, businesses, taxpayers, and politicians. All of these are important to schools as their actions directly or indirectly affect the operations of a school.

Legislatures, colleges, and other governmental or educational agencies increasingly influence schools as well. Administrators must realize that while schools cannot be all things to all constituents, schools depend on their environments for resources and support. School leaders must know who possesses and exercises power in a community. As a group, parents should always receive top priority. This is particularly true in school districts with open enrollment and charter school competition.

It is wise to solicit feedback and identify which expectations have the highest priority within each constituent group. The principal can highlight ways in which the groups' priorities align with the vision and goals already identified. For each identified area, it is important to highlight its level of rigor and the strategy for measuring whether it has been achieved. As each goal is achieved it must be celebrated through the school's public relations campaign.

To determine measurability, the principal must start with the state or district standards and quantify, or assign a numerical value, to the type of performance that meets the expectation. For instance, if students are expected to understand fractions, a measureable expectation would state "at the end of the school year, 90% of second grade students are expected to solve 85% of simple fractions assigned".

Principals must also determine if their school has rigorous expectations. According to the IOWA Core Curriculum Team, there are three attributes of a rigorous educational environment.

- First, instruction must guide students to use higher-order thinking skills to construct knowledge around a central concept or skill. These include Bloom's Taxonomy and its levels of cognition, including the ability to: predict, hypothesize, justify, interpret, synthesize, evaluate, and analyze.
- Second, a rigorous curriculum requires students to demonstrate a deep understanding and mastery of critical disciplinary concepts and skills. Teachers must create assignments that help students gain progressively deeper levels of knowledge of a concept or skill.
- The third attribute is value beyond school. The curriculum must help students think about and apply their knowledge to situations outside of the classroom.

1.2 C   Discriminates between vision and goals that are measurable and non-measurable for all students

Goal setting is instrumental in school growth and improvement. While it is possible to set goals that are broad and not intended to be measured, it is best to select and focus on goals that follow the SMART method. This technique will ensure that effort and resources are devoted to tasks that are achievable and that can be evaluated. It also gives a clear picture of what success will look like.

The SMART method is:

S—Specific
M—Measurable
A—Achievable
R—Relevant
T—Time-framed

When goals are specific, it is easy to evaluate whether or not they have been achieved. The planning process should also identify resources the teachers need or will use to help achieve the goals.

At regular intervals throughout the year, the administrator should meet with each teacher to discuss the goals and how achievement is progressing. The administrator, through visitations to the classroom, will also be able to comment on what is happening and offer advice to the teacher on how to proceed.

While some goals can be accomplished in one school year, some may need to be carried over to the following year.

Skill 1.3   Assures alignments of the vision and goals to school, local, state, and federal policies

Schools must be guided by visions and goals that are aligned with policies set by the district, state, and federal government. Administrators must engage in ongoing professional development to remain cognizant of applicable policies and mandates. School leaders must also facilitate schools reacting to changing environmental conditions, demographics, and economic issues. For instance, changes in the job market require the educational organization to prepare students accordingly. Accommodating these changes must be handled delicately; a school leader can expect difficulties if there is a significant departure from the standards and norms expected in the community.

Schools need to consider not only the immediate community, but also the broader public, governmental regulations, and issues such as declining enrollment and state takeovers. Governmental and public oversight can be seen in the No Child Left Behind (NCLB) legislation originally drafted by the Bush administration in 2001 and then overhauled by the Obama administration in 2010. While this legislation leaves operational policies to local regulation, schools must demonstrate that they successfully prepare all students to meet achievement standards. In many ways, this federal law has encouraged schools to become more competitive with one another for students, attention, and funding.

In describing how NCLB has been updated, on March 15, 2010 the Obama administration released a press release that included the following statement:

"NCLB highlighted the achievement gap and created a national conversation about student achievement. But it also created incentives for states to lower their standards; emphasized punishing failure over rewarding success; focused on absolute scores, rather than recognizing growth and progress; and prescribed a pass-fail, one-size-fits-all series of interventions for schools that miss their goals. The administration's proposal addresses these challenges, while continuing to shine a bright light on closing the achievement gap."

Skill 1.4   Discusses and asks critical questions of key stakeholders about the purposes of education

See Skill 1.4 A and Skill 1.4 B

1.4 A   Formulates appropriate critical questions to ask about the vision and goals

THE DELPHI METHOD

While some stakeholders should be engaged throughout the planning process, others should be brought in after the initial plan has been developed. A good way to engage these individuals is to ask them important questions about the vision and goals that are being proposed. While many strategies can be used, the Delphi method is one that can be particularly useful in an educational setting. Developed by the RAND Corporation in the 1950s, this method uses several rounds of questions and response summaries to obtain a consensus option from a panel of experts. In the Delphi method, anonymity is a key component that eliminates many hindrances of group dynamics such as the halo effect, the bandwagon effect, a reluctance to critique the ideas of others, and unwillingness to revise one's own opinions.

A principal could use the Delphi method to develop a survey about the proposed vision and goals. The administration would collect feedback from diverse stakeholder groups such as staff, parents, and community leaders. When responses were tabulated, another survey would be distributed. It would contain the ratings from the first survey, plus the same or additional questions. After a pre-set number of rounds of questioning, the options with the highest ratings would be considered the best and most adoptable.

See Skill 1.2 B for additional reasons why stakeholders should be included in the decision making.

1.4 B   Polls key stakeholders (i.e., students, teachers, aides, parents, school board members, central office administration, superintendent) about the purposes of education (i.e., develop lifelong learners; develop strong citizens) in relation to vision and goals

The school leader must engage each stakeholder group to meet its needs, determine its perceptions, and leverage its resources. To begin this complex process, the administration should ask questions about how individuals view education and its purposes. Questions should be thought-provoking and should illicit weighty responses. For parents, a critical question may be "what are three things that help you participate in your child's school and what are three things that stop you from participating more in your child's school?" Business owners may be asked "Please give three reasons why you think parents in your neighborhood value education and three reasons why you think they don't value education." In both of these examples, the school leader is asking deductive questions about the respondents' beliefs about education and its purposes.

As highlighted in Skill 1.2, when all groups are engaged, it is easier for rigorous and measurable goals to be implemented, supported, and achieved.

COMPETENCY 002   SHARED COMMITMENTS TO IMPLEMENT THE VISION AND GOALS

Skill 2.1   Engages staff and community members with diverse perspectives to implement the vision and achieve goals

As highlighted in Skill 1.4 A and Skill 1.4 B, stakeholder groups should initially be engaged to provide feedback during the planning process. These individuals and groups can then be supportive as the vision and goals are implemented and achieved. To be effective, communication and cooperative efforts must be open, honest, unbiased, and respectful.

The attitudes of parents and members of the community at large have been adversely affected by reports of the decline of education in the U.S. and negative media coverage. Despite the general perception of the poor quality of public education, the majority of parents surveyed nationally expressed satisfaction with their children's schools and teachers. The most positive feedback resulted when parents felt that their concerns were being heard and addressed and that they were involved in the decision-making process.

This supports the assertion that principals should seek input from parents and other community members in systematic and planned ways. Newsletters, annual surveys, parent nights, and advisory committees allow principals to share information and receive valuable input on a variety of topics. Through these forums, the administration and faculty have opportunities to learn about the community's perception of the school and issues that might have an impact on the school's progress. In addition, the school benefits from individuals who are engaged and are willing to provide resources including their time and expertise.

<u>2.1 A</u>   Identifies individuals with diverse perspectives from the internal and external communities

Within each group of stakeholders, members will have similar concerns and needs; however, in a group, there will also be diverse perspectives. It is important that the school must appreciate and incorporate unique ideas and opinions. Local religious leaders, business owners, neighborhood associations, and day care providers are all important members of the school community. These organizations should have representation on school committees and be members of the school improvement process. Strong relationships with these groups will benefit the school with additional support in the form of funding and programs, as well as support for the school and district initiatives such as referendums.

<u>2.1 B</u>   Identifies strategies to engage internal and external communities with diverse perspectives to implement the vision and goals

Public information management is a systematic communication process that can be used by an educational organization and its public, both within and outside the schools. It is the two-way exchange of information, designed to engage the public in supporting education. The principal competency *concern for image* in the consensus management area specifies that a principal show concern for the school's image. This is accomplished by monitoring the impressions created by students and staff. The principal manages both these impressions and public information communicated about the school by (1) advertising successes, and (2) controlling the flow of negative information.

Public relations must be carefully organized. Information deliverers must have accurate information, understand their roles in disseminating the information, and provide appropriate channels for feedback. The public must perceive that they are being given complete, timely information by officials who respect their feelings and sincerely want feedback. This builds trust and increases the public's commitment to supporting the school and the goals it is working to achieve.

Skill 2.2   Develops shared commitments and responsibilities among staff and the community for selecting and carrying out effective strategies toward the vision and goals

Traditionally, the successful educational leader was recognized as an effective communicator if he or she could persuade subordinates to strive toward challenging goals. Measuring leadership success in these terms resulted in some assumptions; however, current research has shown that the following assumptions *inhibit* effective communication:

- The leader's ideas/goals are viewed as best for the institution. This assumption fosters an authoritative style which discounts the value of ideas generated by employees. Honest feedback is discouraged.

- The setting of goals is the responsibility of an individual or administrative group, not the result of collegial collaboration. This assumption reflects the leadership attitude that employees lack the professional knowledge to participate in the decision-making process.

Post-World War II studies of the social component of work environments revealed that greater communication restraints existed in businesses with rigid social structures that encouraged stereotypical role perceptions. The emphasis on a hierarchical structure fostered low-quality or nonexistent communication between persons who felt inferior and authority figures who perceived themselves as superior.

The development of instructional leadership models in the 1970s was based on traditional assumptions that effective school leaders were firm disciplinarians who set high expectations for employee performance. They set the goals that staff and faculties were expected to meet. However, current thinking suggests that effective schools are lead through building consensus and distributing responsibilities.

2.2 A   Builds consensus

Consensus building is an ideal decision-making tool to use in planning and policy decision making. Reaching a consensus can be a time-consuming art that requires the commitment of all team members. In order to reach consensus, all team members must accept and agree to support the decision at hand. All members may not agree or like the decision, but consensus is met when all members can commit to the decision. Consensus building requires the establishment of group norms and relationship building within the team.

As highlighted in Skill 1.4 A, the Delphi method is one technique for consensus building. When stakeholders are involved in reaching a consensus, these individuals tend to be willing to serve as members of a team. They can be engaged in implementing and achieving the vision, goals, and activities upon which they agreed.

2.2 B   Develops a plan for distributing responsibilities

Studies of human dynamics in the 1980s and 1990s led to total quality management in business and industry. This concept applied to education includes the idea of facilitative leadership, a leadership model which stresses that productive work environments depend on interpersonal relationships that are collaborative and empower all persons involved in the educational process.

The need for power and achievement become shared criteria. The leader focuses on involving employees in problem solving, which leads to improved performance and higher levels of achievement. To share responsibilities, the school leader must engage others and be prepared to provide guidance without undermining the efforts and contributions of other members of the team. The supervisor models positive behaviors that create respect and trust. He or she enhances the staff's individual and group self-concepts through encouragement, constructive criticism, and nonthreatening discipline.

ENCOURAGEMENT

Use the techniques of successful coaches:

- Demonstrate patience and caring. When you are introducing new ideas or information, give staff members the sense that you are constantly considering what is best for the school, the teachers, the support staff, and the students. Referring often to the school's mission, vision, and objectives will keep team efforts focused and give staff members a sense of their role in the organization.

- Take time to explain and demonstrate and give learners ample time to practice. Even professionals cannot be expected to grasp and master new concepts until they have had sufficient time to implement the new skills. To support growth, suggest that those who have learned a new concept observe teachers who have already mastered the expected skills.

- Offer praise and advice. Be sure that praise is sincere and understand that advice is best received when it is warranted and wanted.

- Provide support and positive reinforcement. During the improvement process note specific elements of success and focus on these, not on mistakes.

- Challenge people to do their best. We often settle for less than our full potential. Help team members see an ultimate goal and the steps to its achievement, and then try to be a cheerleader to get them toward the goal.

- Encourage enjoyment and appreciation of work. Work is drudgery when employees do not believe in the product and in their own ability. The coach should help team members realize that doing the work is its own reward. This means that everyone on the team must have the goal clearly in mind, have the ability to strive for the objectives, and participate in activities that are relevant to the goal's accomplishment.

CONSTRUCTIVE CRITICISM

- Lace criticism with deserved, specific, positive praise. To achieve this goal, the supervisor must recognize that individual differences are shaped by societal values and professional attitudes. Planning for constructive criticism requires personal knowledge of performance in the work setting and understanding of each person's interests and emotions. Channeling staff members' creative energies into productive participation reinforces their sense of worth. Make a point to note the value of their contributions orally or in writing. The collective self-concepts of individuals in the school community then contribute to the image of the school.

- Encourage improved performance in a relaxed atmosphere. Severe criticism is threatening and unproductive. It forces the criticized individual or group into a defensive posture. Supervisors should therefore provide opportunities for employees to critique their own performance and offer strategies for improvement.

NONTHREATENING DISCIPLINE

Use effective communication strategies when disciplining employees:

- Improving performance requires putting interventions in place in a timely manner, that is, as soon as the problem is diagnosed.

- Criticize the performance, not the person. Be sure that your personal judgments do not influence your opinions and actions.

- Maintain emotional stability by offering caring support in a courteous manner and voice.

- Address specifics, not generalities. Have your facts straight and adhere to the prescribed method for handling each situation.

- Protect the confidentiality of the diagnoses and interventions.

Skill 2.3   Determines and implements effective strategies to assess and monitor progress toward the vision and goals

To achieve a goal, progress must be monitored and assessed. The entire school community realizes that the leader pays attention and devotes time and resources to those things that are most important. By creating and implementing SMART goals (see Skill 1.2 C.), the administrator highlights the criteria by which everyone can determine success. It is then important for a system to be created, implemented, and monitored.

Monitoring should occur at the beginning of the school year or whenever the vision and goals are first implemented. Throughout the school year the responsible team members should collect and analyze data; the nature of each goal will determine the frequency of its data collection. In many cases, the goal can be discussed and revised even if new data are not available. In order to ensure ongoing progress, the responsible team members should meet, report, and revise the strategy on a weekly or bi-weekly basis. Each team would then report to the school-wide body on a monthly or quarterly basis.

While the principal may decide to wait for the school-wide meeting to obtain updates from the teams, he or she may find it useful to receive reports after each meeting of the individual teams. This will allow the leader to stay abreast of the progress and to provide support whenever a team needs guidance or feedback. This strategy also ensures that the school leader is able to connect the work of all the teams. Regular sub-group reports help the administration to be prepared for the school-wide meeting. The leaders should know what will be said prior to when the teams report to the rest of the staff and definitely before the updates are reported to other members of the community.

Skill 2.4 **Communicates the shared vision and goals in ways that facilitate key stakeholder's ability to understand, support, and act on them**

To engage all stakeholders in working toward the vision and goals, the school leader must communicate in a way that helps individuals understand, support, and act on the plans. Effective communication strategies include good communication practices as well as specific transmission methods.

GOOD COMMUNICATION PRACTICES

- **Think first.** This means preparing for a formal, written, or oral presentation and pausing to gather your thoughts before impromptu speaking.

- **Stay informed.** Never speak or write off-the-cuff or attempt to discuss matters beyond your scope of knowledge. Stay abreast of education issues, especially in leadership and supervision. Read journals and participate in professional organizations. Keep a notebook of newsletters, clippings, and resource lists that can be highlighted and used to add credibility to your communication.

- **Assess your audience.** Know their interests and attitudes. Show respect for their points of view by your tone and pace as well as by your volume and posture when speaking. Demonstrate a genuine liking for people by a willingness to share your ideas and to solicit their responses.

- **Focus attention on your message, not on yourself.** A little nervousness is normal even for practiced writers/speakers. Familiarity with your topic, the ability to develop clear, complete sentences, and the use of concrete examples will enhance delivery.

- **Speak/write correctly.** Use of proper grammar, word choice, and sentence structure will allow listeners/readers to concentrate on what you say rather than on distracting language errors.

- **Be concise.** Get to the point and then quit. Use words and sentences economically. Being unnecessarily long-winded is a sure way to lose your audience.

- **Use delivery techniques to your advantage.** In written communication, be sure to state the main idea, give examples or explanations, and link the ideas in a logical manner. In oral communication, use eye contact to establish sincerity and hold listener attention. Use body language to add enthusiasm and conviction to your words, but avoid expansive or repetitive movements that can distract. Modulate the pitch and volume of your voice for emphasis.

- **Listen thoughtfully to feedback.** In face-to-face communication, be aware of nonverbal cues that suggest either active listening or boredom.

EXAMPLES OF TRANSMISSION METHODS

Written (for internal audiences)

- Daily announcements for students and faculty
- Student newspapers
- Superintendent's monthly newsletter to faculties
- Reports of school board meetings
- Memoranda from all levels, downward or lateral

Written (for external audiences)

- Principal's newsletter to parents
- Emails or e-updates
- Annual reports
- News releases

Oral (for internal audiences)

- Daily announcements or other student broadcasts over intercom or closed circuit television
- Meetings of committees of students, parents, teachers, and administrators
- Faculty meetings
- Student government or club meetings
- Pep rallies

Oral (for external audiences)

- Videotaped promotions of schools or school-related events
- Direct telephone contacts with parents
- Student presentations—concerts, plays, content-area fairs, awards ceremonies
- Radio and television programs to promote school events or discuss educational issues

In any organization or business, good communication is essential. More than half of a school administrator's or supervisor's time is spent communicating with others. The more effective the communication process, the more successful the education process. The administrator's ability to manage the communication process effectively facilitates his or her role as goal setter, task organizer, employee motivator, decision maker, and public relations agent.

2.4 A   Selects the appropriate communication strategies for particular stakeholders

Communication is the exchange of information (message) between a sender and a receiver. The process involves six steps:

1. **Ideating** - development of the idea or message to be communicated.

2. **Encoding** - organization of the idea into a sequence of symbols (written or spoken words, nonverbal cues, or media) to convey the message.

3. **Transmitting** - delivery of the encoded message through a medium (face to face, telephone, written statements, video or computer products).

4. **Receiving** - claiming of the message by the receiver, who must be a good reader/listener and be attentive to the message's meaning.

5. **Decoding** - the receiver's translation of the message.

6. **Acting** - action taken by the receiver in response to the message (ignore, store, react). Communication is reciprocal because the sender must receive feedback that the message has been received and understood.

Educational leadership training programs often explain the communication process in terms of sources and channels. The main source elements are expertise, credibility, composure, and dynamism. The ability to incorporate these elements into idea presentation results in the most persuasive communication.

The means of message transmission are referred to as channels. The characteristics of channels are such elements as the need to use different media for different audiences, the need to use recognizable and respected channels, the need to select mass media that serve different purposes and the recognition of personal channels as more effective than mass media in changing opinions.

DIRECTION OF COMMUNICATION (FORMAL)

1. **Downward** - the transmission of information from people at higher levels to people at lower levels (superintendents to principals, principals to faculty and staff)

2. **Upward** - the transmission of information (usually feedback) from people at lower levels to people at higher levels (principals to directors of instruction, department heads/team leaders to principals)

3. **Lateral (horizontal)** - transmission of information between people on the same level in the organizational structure (assistant superintendent of instruction to assistant superintendent of facilities)

4. **Diagonal** - direct transmission of information between people at different levels in the hierarchy (usually reserved for instances when information cannot go through proper channels in a timely fashion—special reports from principals that go directly to the superintendent or assistant superintendents for transmission to the state)

THE GRAPEVINE

A fifth form of communication exists apart from directional channels—the grapevine. In actuality, the majority of information transmitted by employees laterally is carried through the grapevine. Its face-to-face informality transmits information rapidly.

Administrators should be aware of the school grapevine and incorporate its positive aspects into the communication structure. The negative aspect of unsubstantiated rumor-passing will be overridden if the administrator does the following:

- Keeps employees informed about matters relevant to the school or district and about issues that affect the employees' jobs

- Provides employees the opportunity to express attitudes and feelings about issues

- Tests employees' reactions to information before making decisions

- Builds morale by repeating positive reactions/comments made by employees to higher level administrators or the community and vice versa

Teaching professionals do not like the feeling that they are being kept in the dark or are getting only partial or untimely information. Telling teachers in a faculty meeting that the district is going to reduce the faculty at their school before transfer provisions have been established will create distrust. It may seem an open gesture on the principal's part, but the timing is wrong and the communication will do more harm than good.

ESTABLISHING EFFECTIVE COMMUNICATION

To establish effective communication, the school leader should:

- Establish trust by sincerely correlating his or her message and behavior. For example, claiming an open-door policy but never being available will not create trust.

- Listen carefully and provide open channels for feedback. Avoid giving nonverbal cues that contradict the message.

- Understand and respect employees' needs, interests, and attitudes. Allow discussion, even disagreement. The important thing is that employees know they are being heard.

- Properly time information delivery. Timing affects the manner in which employees perceive the message. Avoid leaking partial information. Transmit accurate information in time for employees to provide feedback.

- Use appropriate media for transmitting the message. Written or face-to-face communication is necessary when the message is of concern to a single receiver or when the message is of immediate concern to a group with common interests. Oral or video presentations are appropriate for delivery of information that affects a department or faculty, such as safety measures or procedures for reporting abuse.

2.4 B   Assesses the effectiveness of communication strategies

The communication process requires that the sender and receiver have a common frame of reference. Administrators must assess the effectiveness of their communication strategies and should then revise them as necessary. The leader should solicit honest feedback about the impact and message that was received from communication shared with constituents. In addition, the leader must realize that each person interprets information based on previous experience and cultural background; therefore, receivers may interpret a message differently than the sender intended. For example, information delivered during contract negotiations may be interpreted differently by union representatives than by district contract negotiators.

These different perceptions arise because the participants are operating from different frames of reference. These differences can be overcome when the groups recognize that they are working toward a common goal. For instance in the case of the contract negotiations, all parties must realize that the specific goal of the negotiation is not to deprive either group but to allocate funds in the most educationally sound manner.

Filtering is a barrier that occurs during transmission of information from one level to another. It may be intentional or unintentional. In downward communication, it may be the omission of some of the message or improper encoding for the intended audience. Administrators frequently deliver information only on a need-to-know basis or deliver only positive information, fearing that negative information will damage the decoding process. This succeeds only in causing the receivers to be confused about the message's intent or to feel patronized. In upward communication, employees may limit information to those facts that shed favorable light on their personal performance because of previous experience with inconsistent or arbitrary evaluations.

Improper listening skills also interfere with communication. The receiver must heed the entire message, decode it non-judgmentally, and seek clarification of any unclear points. This happens best when the sender creates a nonthreatening environment in which the listener can practice non-evaluative listening.

Biases against race, gender, or status can prejudice receivers against a message. Senders can suggest bias by words, nonverbal clues, or attitudes. A male principal with chauvinist attitudes may alienate female teachers; and likewise a female principal may alienate male teachers through unintended actions and comments.

Skill 2.5   Implements the shared vision and goals consistently

Consistency is a key requirement for success. To achieve the vision and goals, a school leader must consistently reinforce the changes needed to overcome persistent barriers within the system. *Organizational development* is a values-based approach to systems change. The goal is to build the capacity to achieve and sustain a new desired state that benefits the organization and community around it. It is an evolving field of practice grounded in a set of core values and principles that guide behavior and actions.

Key values of this approach include:

- **Respect and inclusion**, equitably valuing the perspective and opinions of everyone;

- **Collaboration**, building collaborative relationships between the stakeholders while encouraging collaboration throughout the system;

- **Authenticity**, striving for authenticity and congruence and encouraging these qualities in everyone;

- **Self-awareness**, committing to developing self-awareness and interpersonal skills.

- Personal and professional development are achieved through lifelong learning and **Empowerment**, focusing efforts on helping everyone in the community increase their autonomy and empowerment to levels that make the workplace and/or community satisfying and productive.

Organizational development draws from multiple disciplines that inform an understanding of human systems, including applied behavioral and physical sciences. It approaches communities and organizations as open systems, with the knowledge that change in one area of a system always results in changes in other areas, and change in one area cannot be sustained without supporting changes in other areas of the system. This approach encourages continuously reexamining, reflecting upon, and integrating discoveries throughout the change process in order to achieve desired outcomes. In this way, individuals are involved both in doing their work and, to achieve shared results, in reflection and dialogue about their learning. Tools include survey feedback, assessment tools, interviewing, focus groups, storytelling, process consultation, and observation.

COMPETENCY 003   **CONTINUOUS IMPROVEMENT TOWARD THE VISION AND GOALS**

Skill 3.1   **Uses a data system and multiple sources of data to conduct a needs analysis to identify unique strengths, needs, gaps, and areas of improvement for students and teachers**

A needs assessment is a wise first initial step in program or curriculum planning. It provides the opportunity to survey stakeholders and identify the context in which the program will be developed. The needs assessment survey should focus primarily on the needs of the students. This focus can identify achievement problems so goals can be written for the initial planning stage and specific instructional objectives can be formulated.

Systematic assessment of school needs may range from grade-level surveys of needs to school-wide surveys. This practice will not have full impact unless careful attention is given to how it relates to the cohesive set of visions and goals developed jointly with administrators, teachers, parents, and members of the school community. It is important that the instrument gathers pertinent data and information related to students' needs and the program environment at the school. Once the instrument is administered and the results are quantified, analyzed, and interpreted, the direction to follow is then determined.

When the purpose of the needs assessment is for program development, goal statements are carefully stated and established, and goals are prioritized and linked to performance outcomes of the students. High-priority goals are implemented with specific strategies delineated. However, if the purpose of the assessment is to check progress, then the assessment instrument should reflect statements concerning activities and functions of the students and the staff, as well communication among the various levels. The systematic assessment of school needs should go beyond surveys to include students' cumulative folder contents, anecdotal records, test results, interviews, classroom sociograms, direct teacher observations, and other means deemed appropriate.

Skill 3.2   **Uses data-driven decision making, research, and best practices to shape and monitor plans, programs, and activities to achieve the vision and goals**

Proactive and transformative administrative teams consistently foster an environment with excellence in standards and expectations for both students and staff. This is done through decision making processes that are guided by school-based data, current educational research, and knowledge of best practices that can be emulated. Researchers have consistently suggested that administrators and other stakeholders create norms and values that promote school performance excellence. They have found that these values are transmitted through instructional practices, students and staff, and ultimately affect learning performance. Visionary administrators understand that effective teachers facilitate productive learners who are eager to apply new knowledge in the classroom and in their life experiences.

Administrators must be knowledgeable about effective teaching practices and what is working (and not working) in every classroom, for every teacher, and ultimately for every student. Gaining this knowledge may require research and visiting schools that are working for students. Schools that demonstrate high standardized test scores and that exemplify the vision of NCLB can provide quantifiable knowledge of what's working in classrooms for both staff and students. Effective teaching and learning must include rigor, relevancy, and relationship of materials. Administrators must support positive community relationships that personalize the school environment for staff, students, parents, and other members of the learning community. Through professional development, administrators can learn the latest research-based strategies for achieving the school's vision and goals.

Skill 3.3 Identifies and addresses barriers to achieving the vision and goals

Previous skills have highlighted the importance of stakeholder buy-in, data analysis, and constant communication and planning. These steps will help identify and remove many barriers to achieving the vision and goals. Another important factor is motivation; which has been defined by Baron (1992) as a force that energizes, sustains, and channels behavior toward a goal. Individuals have needs, desires, likes, and dislikes and these are related to their motivation; thus, an effective leader must understand motivation and how it relates to goal attainment.

MOTIVATIONAL STRATEGIES

Theorists maintain that there are two types of motivation: *intrinsic* motivation, which results from an individual's internal drive, and *extrinsic* motivation, which is influenced by incentives and rewards external to the individual. A number of theories have been developed to explain what influences individuals to work enthusiastically, to want to engage in professional growth, to contribute to goal attainment in organizations, and to act responsibly. According to Hoy and Miskel (1996), motivating individuals is a complex process of trying to facilitate desired motivational patterns. One strategy to influence motivation is providing for the needs, desires, and likes of individuals in an organizational setting; this in turn has an impact on the objectives of the organization.

Cognitive and Humanistic Approaches to Motivation
Using reinforcers to influence behavior then becomes an important element in motivational theory, specifically, the behavioral approach. The two other categories of motivation are the *cognitive* and *humanistic approaches*. While the behavioral approach to motivation suggests that motivation depends on the effectiveness of reinforcers, cognitive theory suggests that motivation consists of two personal factors, expectations and beliefs (Eggen and Kauchak, 1997). When there is the expectation that one can succeed at a task, and value is attached to achieving that task, then a feeling of self-efficacy emerges. In organizations, then, leaders may ask what can be

done to help bring about emotions of self-efficacy in their members. The humanistic perspective views motivation as attempts by people to reach their potential (Eggen and Kauchak, 1997). Motivation proceeds from internal mechanisms acting to cause individuals to achieve, grow and develop, and reach their potential.

Environmental Factors in Motivation
Incentives and rewards are used by an organization to influence the motivation of its members, thus making them more productive. Of importance in any work environment are the environmental factors present, those things that tend to make the workplace enjoyable and those things that tend to make the workplace distasteful. An administrator's attention to these factors permeates the workplace and, subsequently, has an impact on the motivation of members to accomplish tasks and fulfill organizational goals.

The term "educational accountability" sometimes means that educational policies rely on the idea of external motivation to improve instructional quality. In its original form NCLB operated largely on the principle that rewards and punishments would increase motivational levels of teachers, principals, and students. Growth targets were incremental; however, when they were not met, punishments were imposed on individual teachers, administrators, or entire schools.

This attempt at external motivation was refined in 2010 into an ESEA blueprint that promises to reward outstanding teachers and leaders and recognize schools that exhibit student progress. Irrespective of what is promised at higher levels of the educational system, whether federal, state, or district, an educational leader can remove motivational barriers at his or her level. One effective strategy is to engage teachers, staff, parents, students, and other members of the community. Engagement facilitates the intrinsic motivation that occurs when stakeholders believe that the school's vision and goals support their own personal or career-related visions and goals.

Wise leaders also realize that it is important for educational success to be recognized and celebrated in a very public way. There should be at least one annual event during which the school celebrates the hard work put in by students, teachers and staff, parents, businesses, and community supporters. At some schools there is an assembly each month and this provides an opportunity for one class, teacher, and community person to be spotlighted. This monthly practice can serve as motivation for people to give their greatest effort while awaiting their turn for recognition. By the end of the year, all stakeholders will have had an opportunity to be recognized.

Skill 3.4   Implements effective strategies to facilitate needed change

Change is a difficult process that is not always welcomed but that can be facilitated. George Bernard Shaw noted that "reformers have the idea that change can be achieved by brute sanity". While educational systems are more open than most and are therefore more prone to challenging change efforts, research has shown that some strategies can help facilitate needed changes. An important one is data gathering that gives meaning to what is being measured. By involving all stakeholders in the early phases of program reform, it is easier to gain buy-in and support for the changes that need to be made.

PHASES OF DATA COLLECTION

Ornstein and Hunkins (1993) identify five distinct phases for gathering data to assess and improve upon program effectiveness. These include *identifying* the curriculum phenomena to be evaluated and *collecting*, *organizing*, *analyzing*, and *reporting* and *recycling* the data. In the first phase, identifying the curriculum phenomena to be evaluated, the evaluator determines the design of the evaluation and specifies exactly what will be evaluated. The evaluators determine if the entire school will be included or just selected grade levels or subject areas. Whatever is decided at this stage must include a clear delineation of the relationship among the variables. This includes establishing a clear relationship among the objectives, the constraints of the learning activities, and the expected outcomes.

In the collection phase, the evaluator must identify the sources of information; this is based on the design established in the previous phase. A plan must be developed to collect hard data from various sources including parents, teachers, staff, students, and other members of the school community. Organizing the information leads the evaluator to arrange the data so that it is usable. This includes coding and storing the data in a system where it can be retrieved for analysis. The data are then analyzed based on statistical approaches that are suitable for the information collected.

Reporting the information requires the evaluator to determine the level of formality that will meet the needs of the various audiences. Finally, recycling the information shows that evaluation is a continuous process. The implication is that the information received from this process will provide feedback for program modification and adjustment, which will lead to continuous change in an organization that is itself continuously changing.

The implementation process must be strategically planned with benchmarks to determine specific levels of program goal attainment leading to the reexamination of the strategies being used for specific learning outcomes. When placed on a time line, the benchmarks may also serve as pointers for communicating with various audiences. Feedback from the various sources must be used to determine the extent to which the goals and expected outcomes are being achieved. This information will supply the agenda items to be acted upon and hence the plan drives the implementation, dissemination, and change processes.

Skill 3.5   Engages staff and community stakeholders in planning and carrying out programs and activities

See Skill 2.2 A and Skill 2.2 B

Skill 3.6   Aligns planning, change strategies and instructional programs with the vision and goals

The instructional program includes the school curriculum and is the action plan to educate children. These must be aligned with the planning and change strategies that the school or system will use to achieve its vision and goals. At the local level, change is effected by data including achievement data, report cards, and anecdotal records kept by teachers. Other sources of information include attitudinal surveys of the students, teachers, and parent and community groups.

The nation is also concerned with producing citizens who are prepared to transmit the ideals of a democratic society. Therefore, the school as a societal institution must align its teaching and learning processes to produce these desirable learner outcomes. The design of the curriculum accounts for the way the elements of the curriculum are organized. Although many school districts have begun to adopt pre-designed "boxed" curricula, educational leaders must still be familiar with curriculum design and theories of learning. This knowledge assists the administrator in helping teachers and staff to deliver effective instruction and maximize student learning.

THEORIES OF LEARNING

Curriculum selection must also take into account contributions from the field of psychology, which is responsible for the major theories of learning. Learning theories serve as the foundation for methods of teaching, materials for learning, and activities that are age- and developmentally- appropriate for learning. Major theories of learning include behaviorism, cognitive development, and phenomenology, or humanistic psychology.

Behaviorism emphasizes conditioning the behavior of the learner and altering the environment to obtain specific responses. As one of the oldest theories of learning, behaviorism focuses specifically on stimulus-response and reinforcement for learning. The work of Thorndike led to the development of connectionism theories, from which came the laws of learning:

- **Law of Readiness:** Students learn best when they are ready to learn. Successful cognitive growth occurs when new information builds upon previously mastered content.

- **Law of Exercise:** A connection is strengthened based on the proportion to the number of times it occurs, its duration, and its intensity.

- **Law of Effect:** Responses accompanied by satisfaction strengthen the connection while responses accompanied by dissatisfaction weaken the connection.

These laws also influenced the curriculum contributions of Ralph Tyler, Hilda Taba, and Jerome Bruner, who discarded the view of specific stimuli and responses to endorse broader views of learning. For example, Taba recognized that practice alone does not transfer learning; therefore, rote learning and memorization should not be emphasized.

Jerome Bruner, on the other hand, contributed the notion that learning is better transferred when students learn structure rather than by rote memorization. *Classical conditioning* theories emphasized the elicit-response aspect of learning through adequate stimuli. Pavlov and Watson taught a dog to salivate at the sound of a bell. This was accomplished by presenting food simultaneously with a stimulus, the bell. Their experiment gave rise to the notion that the learner could be conditioned for learning or training, a theory that could be applied to any profession.

Operant conditioning is a behavioral theory promoted by B. F. Skinner. It emphasizes learning by following behavior with either positive or negative reinforcers. This theory uses reinforcers to increase desirable behavior and "punishments" to decrease unwanted behavior. Positive reinforcers give desirable stimuli and negative reinforcers take away unpleasant stimuli. In contrast, positive punishment gives unpleasant stimuli and negative punishment removes desirable stimuli.

Behavioral theories gave birth to behavior-modification approaches to discipline and learning. Albert Bandura's theory of observational learning and modeling focuses on children learning through modeling the behaviors of others. The *hierarchical learning theories* of Robert Gagne organize types of learning into a classical, hierarchical model of intellectual skills, information, cognitive strategies, motor skills, and attitudes learned through positive experiences.

Cognitive development theories focus on human growth and development in terms of cognitive, social, psychological, and physical development. These theories suggest that schools should not focus solely on children's cognitive development. The *developmental theories* of Jean Piaget propose that growth and development occur in stages. Piaget identified four stages of development: the sensory-motor stage (birth to age 2), in which the child manipulates the physical surroundings; the preoperational stage (ages 2-7), in which complex learning takes place through experiences; the concrete operational stage (ages 7-11), in which the child organizes information in logical forms using concrete objects; and the formal operational stage (age 11 and above), in which the child can perform formal and abstract operations.

Phenomenology, or humanistic psychology, is not widely recognized as a school of psychology; those who disregard it believe that psychology in and of itself is humanistic in nature, therefore, there is no need for such a school. However, those who believe in the theory regard it as a third school because it emphasizes the person as a total organism during the learning process rather than separating learning into the domains of behavior and cognition. *Gestalt psychology* is representative of phenomenology and humanistic psychology. It represents wholeness as recognized in Maslow's hierarchy of needs, in which the end product is a wholesome, happy, and healthy child/person who is self-actualized and fulfilled. The various theories of learning have served as foundations on which curricular decisions have been made.

The school curriculum should satisfy societal needs and goals to produce individuals who have the social, intellectual, moral, emotional and civic development to function as an integral part of our democratic society. However, selecting the best curriculum to meet all of these needs is not an easy task. It should be a collaborative effort and necessary changes should be clearly rationalized to meet existing district and school goals. This clarity should explain the new subject structure and content and the needs of the students regarding ability, performance, level of success, and instructional strategies. Administrators should also consider the motivation of students and instructional staff, feasibility of time and resources, and curriculum balance in terms of concepts, skills, and application.

Also see Skill 5.4 A

3.6 A   Outlines a process and criteria to show how planning, change strategies, and instructional programs support the vision and goals

To successfully implement a new vision, set of goals, instructional program, or curriculum, the school must engage in careful planning. Communication during the implementation process is essential, especially when changes will upset the status quo. The channels of communication must always be open so that discussion and exchange are ongoing at all levels and across groups. Effective communication requires high quality exchange through two-way channels within a defined network. While the formal network remains the official way of communicating in organizations, the informal network should not be ignored or discouraged. It can be shaped into a very healthy system of communication between members of the organization.

School restructuring often calls for communication models other than the traditional top-down approach. Informal lateral communication might be a small group of teachers deciding among themselves to get together and share ideas from an article that could be useful in their classrooms. Formal lateral communications may be written and disseminated in a systematic way through newsletters, bulletins, memos, and reports. It may also be verbal and transmitted through speeches, lectures, and oral reports where body language, tone of voice, and other physical expressions can enhance the message being communicated.

The mode of communication should be adjusted to meet the needs of the audience. For instance, teachers may expect in-service trainings where well-defined educational terms are used and specific strategies are developed or practiced. In contrast, a presentation for parents, community groups, and other lay individuals should be free of educational jargon and adjusted to the participants' educational levels and school experiences. Whatever the mode or approaches to communication, a steady flow of information exchange at every stage of program implementation is necessary.

Skill 3.7   Aligns all resources, including technology, to achieve the vision and goals

One of the major impediments to establishing successful computer-based applications in schools is the lack of careful and extensive planning (Picciano, 1998). Kearsley (1995) wrote that school leaders must be able to identify how computers can improve the efficiency of school operations. He stated that a school leader must plan computer use so that it serves the interests and needs of all school constituents. A specific list of competencies is associated with school leaders' ability to make policy decisions governing the use of technological resources.

A school leader must have knowledge of computer terminology, instructional and administrative applications, and the impact of technology in the school environment. An essential ingredient of good administration is planning. He or she must plan for all aspects of integrating technology in a school. The determination of which hardware and software to acquire is essential in the process, as is the identification of goals and objectives. To ensure that computer implementation proceeds without problems, it is important to have policy statements and procedures governing its use.

The introduction of technology in a learning environment should not be based on technology for technology's sake, but rather on a calculated and planned agenda in which its use is aligned to achieve the specified vision and goals. A learning environment characterized by technology offers a unique mode of instruction and interaction. It is a student-centered, constructivist model, where students are challenged to engage in higher-order thinking, interact with technology at their own level, and learn what interests them.

<u>3.7 A</u>   Outlines a process and criteria to demonstrate how resources support achievement of the vision and goals

School leaders are charged with providing students and staff with resources that support achievement of the vision and goals such as a rigorous academic learning environment. In all resource areas, it is important for the principal to build relationships with the employees so that there is open dialogue concerning what is best for the children and the school. It is important that employees in all departments, including food service, maintenance, and transportation, are included in the planning and decision making for the school. It is also important to include these staff as members of the school community by having them participate in activities and celebrations. They often go unnoticed but are important resources in the effective operation of the school.

Skill 3.8   **Monitors evidence about progress systematically and revises plans, programs, and activities as needed**

See Skill 2.5

3.8 A   **Develops a process that systematically monitors progress towards the vision and goals**

See Skill 2.3

DOMAIN II TEACHING AND LEARNING

COMPETENCY 004   BUILDING A PROFESSIONAL CULTURE

Skill 4.1   Develops a shared understanding of and commitment to high standards for all students and closing achievement gaps

4.1 A   Creates a culture of high expectations for all students

Students are at varying stages of development in any grade. When the administration has high expectations and supports teachers in applying appropriate pedagogy, students are challenged and enriched at every level. To create these challenging and enriching experiences, high expectations must be the norm. This includes showing students and parents that academic requirements must be met or consequences will be enforced. For instance, when assignments are due, they must be submitted in a timely fashion. Educators must emphasize that high expectations are in place to prepare students for their future as productive citizens. Assignments should challenge students and lead them to an understanding of how their in-class learning is applicable to real world situations. This conveys the highest expectation of all—the belief that each student will have an important and positive role in society and that he or she must learn as much as possible in order to be prepared for this role.

To be effective and achievable, the expectations must be appropriate for the ages and developmental levels of the students. Therefore, the administrator of the school should have knowledge of the developmental stages that children go through to be knowledgeable about the curricular outcomes and types of learning activities teachers can plan. These domains include children's intellectual, social, emotional, physical, spiritual, and moral development.

Intellectually, kindergarten students are curious and eager to learn. They are interested in books and stories and love to be actively involved. They are lively and constantly in motion, but depending on their individual circumstances, they may not be very well developed socially or emotionally. The spiritual and moral development of children before they come to school also depends on their family situations. At this stage, children need a lot of extra support with literacy and numeracy.

As students progress through the grades, teachers and administrators are able to see growth in all areas. The administrator knows that although elementary grade children like to think they are grown up, they still act their age and do childish things. The instruction that teachers provide in the classroom should include ongoing modeling. At this developmental stage, students do not remember directions and need to have them written down. They are active because they are still growing, so it is common to find them racing around. They need time in the gym or outdoors. Most elementary school students have become fluent readers, but there may still be some who are struggling. When students have problems with reading, it usually results in problems in other subjects.

At the junior high level, students are not quite so active physically; however, they are more mentally mature and teachers can engage them in frank classroom discussions. They like to experiment, so disciplinary problems tend to increase in this age group. These students are fairly independent in their study habits, but there will be groups of students who still need support or who need to be prodded into completing their work.

In the high school years, students become more independent learners. By this time, struggling students can choose to take different courses of study; however, supports must still be provided in school.

4.1 B   Identifies achievement gaps

Achievement gaps are best identified by reviewing assessment data. One type of gap exists when a student does not exhibit the knowledge that he or she is expected to have. For example, there is an achievement gap when a second grade student does not master the math concepts that he or she should know. A second type of gap is one that exists when different groups of students exhibit different levels of knowledge. These achievement gaps are sometimes referred to as performance disparities between student-groupings. Grouping designations include race/ethnicity, gender, and socio-economic variables such as parental income and educational levels.

See Skill 1.1 B for more information on various types of assessments.

4.1 C   Develops plans to reduce gaps

Administrators and teachers must recognize that disparities, or performance differences, have long been a challenge in education. Effective and equitable schools work to reduce and eliminate these gaps. They do this, not by lowering standards for higher performing groups, but by analyzing performance data, identifying areas that need specific focus and planning, and teaching with the purpose of enhancing learning for all students.

No two students are alike. It follows, then, that no students learn alike. To apply a one-dimensional instructional approach and have strict tunnel vision is to impose learning limits on students. All students have the right to an education, but there cannot be a singular path to that education. Administrators must acknowledge the variety of learning styles and abilities among students from class to class and within each class. To reduce learning gaps, teachers must be supported in applying multiple methods of assessment and instruction.

To apply this strategy effectively, additional staff or volunteers will need to be available during instructional time. While the teacher works with re-teaching or using a different instructional method, other adults can work with those students who have mastered the concept. When additional "bodies" are not available, teachers may be able to provide independent learning activities so that advanced students can work on their own. Then the teacher can focus on instructing those students who still need to understand the concept. In this way every child has appropriate opportunities to master the subject matter, demonstrate such mastery, and improve and enhance learning skills with each lesson.

Skill 4.2   Guides and supports job-embedded, standards based professional development that meets the learning needs of all students and staff

Professional development is a crucial component of successful school change. New standards and accountability systems demand much more of teachers than ever before, and many teachers simply do not have the skills or knowledge to implement the many requirements for which they are now responsible.

Significant research on professional development has concluded that among the worst ways of helping teachers learn new skills or knowledge is putting them through a "one-shot" staff in-service training session. This is a session that focuses on a particular strategy or technique for the classroom. Sometimes these sessions are one to two hours long. Other times, they are five to six hours long. In either case, these sessions give teachers no reason to utilize their new learning, nor do they take into account adult learning theory. Adult learning theory suggests that adults learn best when they have an immediate application of their learning. Since most staff in-services have no follow-up (discussion about how the strategy worked, one-on-one coaching, etc.), most teachers will not try the new strategies. After all, they feel safe and comfortable with their current procedures.

Effective professional development consists of deep learning across time with significant opportunities for follow-up, discussion, assistance, and reflection. Often, when professional development sessions on one topic are spread out over a whole year (e.g., one three-hour session per month), teachers have more reason to follow through with trying new ideas in the classroom.

When schools add components of professional learning communities—group configurations that allow for discussion of new learning—then teachers have more opportunity to reflect upon, discuss, and question the new ideas. This allows teachers to work through personal concerns and problems they might be facing in their classrooms.

Consistently, teachers report in surveys that they never have enough time to learn new strategies. Therefore, it is crucial that professional development not be limited to just a couple of hours per year. Schools must provide teachers with multiple opportunities, often by rearranging the school day, so that teachers can interact with each other and with new teaching ideas on a more regular basis.

4.2 A   Develops processes to support teacher's growth and interests to support student learning

To support and motivate teachers, administrators can use intrinsic or extrinsic strategies; these are discussed in greater detail in Skill 3.3.

Intrinsic motivation is when a person is motivated by internal factors as opposed to external factors. Intrinsic motivation drives people to do things because they are fun or because they believe they are a good or right thing to do. Intrinsic motivation is much stronger than extrinsic motivation. For many educators, teaching is their passion and they are intrinsically motivated to help their students learn and do well. School leaders can support intrinsic motivation by recognizing when teachers work hard and by encouraging them to do so.

Extrinsic motivation is motivation by external factors. It drives people to do things for tangible rewards or because of outside pressures rather than for the fun of it. Staff members are often motivated by their salary, bonuses, or sanctions imposed for not achieving certain mandates.

Research has shown that extrinsic motivation is not the most effective method to be used if a school wants to have a strong learning community. If extrinsic motivators are used initially, they must be accompanied by strategies that build intrinsic motivation. Then as the intrinsic motivation increases, the extrinsic strategies are removed.

For more information on motivation, see Skill 3.3

4.2 B   Analyzes situations and recommends appropriate teaching and learning practices

The principal does not need to be a subject-matter expert, nor does he or she have to possess all the answers to issues of classroom management. However, to engage the best support staff, the school leader must be aware of basic pedagogical concepts. For instance, the principal should be able to analyze test scores and realize that when students are performing at vastly different levels, an instructional specialist needs to be brought in. This is a professional who can help teachers create a plan for individualizing instruction. Likewise, an assessment specialist or special education support-staff member can facilitate the collection of effective assessment data from students with special needs. A few important instructional techniques are listed below. School leaders should be aware of how teachers exhibit understanding and mastery of these techniques. Then the administrator can support teachers if they are not proficient in these areas.

DIFFERENTIATED INSTRUCTION

It is difficult to define intelligence, but teachers know and recognize the differences in the intelligence of their students. This complicates the development of *differentiated instruction* (DI). Some of the children from homes where reading, books, and learning are not a high priority will, nevertheless, rank high on the intelligence scale as will some where parents seem indifferent to their children's progress. Some will be very low on this scale regardless of background. It is very challenging to develop teaching approaches and methods that will make certain none of the children are left behind. Should a teacher choose the lowest common denominator and ignore the likelihood that many of the students in the class could grasp highly abstract ideas and concepts, or is it better to aim for the middle and hope for the best?

Accepting Students' Differences

A committed educator not only accepts students' differences but also acts on them by differentiating his or her instructional practices. This means that differentiating instruction is not something done on Fridays; it is what effective teachers do every day in the classroom so that every student's learning needs are met. According to well-respected DI proponent Carol Ann Tomlinson, differentiation "occurs as teachers become increasingly proficient in understanding their students as individuals, increasingly comfortable with the meaning and structure of the disciplines they teach, and increasingly expert at teaching flexibly in order to match instruction to student need with the goal of maximizing the potential of each learner in a given area."

Understanding Students

Teachers who differentiate their instruction begin by developing a broad and thorough understanding of their students. Gathering this data about students and using it to purposefully implement differentiated practices can be time consuming and cumbersome, especially as greater demands and expectations squeeze into teachers' already tight schedules. However, by promoting the focused and deliberate integration of technology, these challenging and sometimes difficult tasks can become both practical and increasingly more manageable in the differentiated classroom.

Implementing DI in the Classroom

The effective teacher will seek to connect all students to the subject matter through multiple techniques, with the goal that each student, through their own abilities, will relate to one or more techniques and excel in the learning process. Differentiated instruction encompasses several areas:

- **Content:** What is the teacher going to teach? Or, perhaps better put, what does the teacher want the students to learn? Differentiating content means that students will have access to content that piques their interest about a topic, with a complexity that provides an appropriate challenge for their intellectual development.

- **Process:** This is a classroom management technique where instructional organization and delivery is maximized for the diverse student group. These techniques should include dynamic, flexible grouping activities, where instruction and learning occurs as whole-class units, teacher-led activities, and peer learning and teaching (while teacher observes and coaches) within small groups or pairs.

- **Product:** There are expectations and requirements placed on students to demonstrate their knowledge or understanding. The type of product expected from each student should reflect each student's own capabilities.

COOPERATIVE LEARNING

Cooperative learning situations, as practiced in today's classrooms, grew out of research studies in the early 1970s. Cooperative learning situations can range from very formal applications such as *Student Teams-Achievement Divisions (STAD)* and *Cooperative Integrated Reading and Composition (CIRC)* to less formal groupings known variously as *group investigation, learning together*, or *discovery groups*. **Cooperative learning** as a general term is now firmly recognized and established as a teaching and learning technique in American schools.

Implementing Cooperative Learning in the Classroom

Cooperative learning techniques are widely diffused in schools; therefore, it is necessary to orient students in the skills by which cooperative learning groups can operate smoothly, and thereby enhance learning. Students who cannot interact constructively with other students will not be able to take advantage of the learning opportunities provided by the cooperative learning situations and will furthermore deprive their fellow students of the opportunity for cooperative learning. These skills form the hierarchy of cooperation in which students first learn to work together as a group, they may then proceed to levels at which they may engage in simulated-conflict situations. This cooperative setting allows different points of view to be entertained constructively.

ALTERNATIVE ASSESSMENTS

Alternative assessments allow students to create an answer or a response to a question or task. This is as opposed to traditional, inflexible assessments where students choose a response from among a prepared selection, such as matching, multiple-choice, or true/false. Efforts to develop useful alternatives to standardized testing have proliferated during the past several years. Few current movements have caught the attention of educators as quickly as the move toward more direct assessment of student performance.

Several labels have been used to describe alternatives to standardized tests. The most common include *direct assessment, authentic assessment, performance assessment*, and the more generic *alternative assessment*. Proponents feel that sampling tiny snippets of student behavior does not provide insight into how students would perform on truly worthy intellectual tasks and that student learning can be better assessed by examining and judging a student's actual (or simulated) performance on significant, relevant tasks.

Implementing Alternative Assessments in the Classroom

When implemented effectively, an alternative assessment approach will exhibit these characteristics, among others:

- Requires higher-order thinking and problem-solving
- Provides opportunities for student self-reflection and self-assessment
- Uses real world applications to connect students to the subject
- Provides opportunities for students to learn and examine subjects on their own, as well as to collaborate with their peers.
- Encourages students to continuing learning beyond the requirements of the assignment
- Clearly defines objective and performance goals

TESTING MODIFICATIONS

The intent of testing modifications is to minimize the effect of a student's disability or learning challenge. This provides an equal opportunity for students with disabilities to participate in assessments to demonstrate and express their knowledge and ability.

Testing modifications should be identified in the student's IEP, consistently implemented, and used to the least extent possible. Types of testing modifications include:

- **Flexible scheduling**: providing time extensions or altering testing duration (e.g., by inserting appropriate breaks).
- **Flexible setting**: using special lighting or acoustics, minimizing distractions (e.g., testing the student in a separate location), using adaptive equipment.
- **Alternate test format**: using large print or Braille, increasing the space allocated for student response, realigning the format of question and answer selections (e.g., vertically rather than horizontally).
- **Use of mechanical aids**: tape recorders, word processors, visual and auditory magnification devices, calculators, spell check and grammar check software (where spelling and grammar are not the focus of the assessment).

Skill 4.3   Models openness to change and collaborative processes

Successful administrators share leadership and they are open about the need for change. They reach out to teachers, staff, parents, and the community. Such leaders work hard to expand the professional capacity of their teachers to develop a coherent professional community. Effective leaders have the same set of standards for themselves and others. They embrace change, create energy, bring harmony, forge consensus, set high standards, and develop a "try this" orientation to the future. They are forever hopeful and cause everyone in the school's community to share this hope. When this type of environment exists, everyone is willing to engage in the hard work that is necessary for effective changes to be made.

4.3 A   Collaborates with all stakeholders to discuss the need for change

When an educational leader has engaged in careful planning and research he or she may determine that change is necessary. The next step is to collaborate with his/her direct reports in order to present the facts, highlight the leader's ideas, and solicit feedback and buy-in. After these individuals are engaged, it may be necessary to engage upward stakeholders, such as district staff members and/or the superintendent. If the leader operates at the district level such as if he or she is the superintendent, then upward stakeholders may include staff at the state's Department of Education. Downward stakeholders would always include teachers, support staff, parents, and students.

If it is at the school level, these individuals can be solicited as a whole group with open meetings or self-selected committees. At the district level or higher, these constituents should come from organizations such as the teachers' unions, Parent Teacher Association (PTA), and district-wide or cross-school student council(s). It is important that all pertinent stakeholders are engaged as soon as the change effort begins. Early collaboration makes it much easier for changes to be planned, supported, and achieved.

4.3 B   Demonstrates a willingness to change own position on an issue

Transparency is important in a collaborative environment. With transparency comes the need for honesty; which then creates a need for problem-solving skills. School leaders must show that they can be trusted, that they do not hold double-standards for themselves or others, and that they are willing to devote the energy and time necessary for truly democratic practices.

When evidence supports the need for change, the leader must be ready to alter his or her position or policy. Once again, open communication is critical; as changes are made, stakeholders must be informed and updated. In this way, the school community will understand that the leadership values them and wants to make sure they are aware of important changes.

Skill 4.4   Creates structures, procedures, and relationships that provide time and resources for a collaborative teaching and learning community

See Skill 4.4 A, 4.4 B, and 4.4 C

<u>**4.4 A**</u>   **Promotes mutual benefits and distribution of responsibility and accountability among the teaching and learning community**

Schools are open social systems, as such they are impacted by individual and group dynamics. This is particularly the case when the school operates collaboratively and all stakeholders are to participate, be held accountable, and share in the responsibilities and benefits of the teaching and learning community. When problems arise, the school leader can use them as opportunities to promote the benefits of having a collaborative school environment.

Hersey and Blanchard (1988) identified four group problem-solving modes: (1) crisis mode (2) organizational mode (3) interpersonal mode, and (4) routine procedural mode. As presented in the table below, the situational leadership model emphasizes task behavior and relationship behavior to resolve organizational problems.

	High Relationship	**Low Relationship**
High Task Behavior	Organizational Mode	Crisis Mode
Low Task Behavior	Interpersonal Mode	Routine Mode

In their model for problem solving, Parnes, Noller, and Biondi (1977) developed a five-step approach: (1) fact finding (2) problem finding (3 idea finding (4) solution finding, and (5) acceptance finding. Fact finding centers on gathering information related to a situation. Problem finding identifies the problems and sub-problems. Idea finding employs techniques to create ideas about the problem. Solution finding uses criteria to evaluate the ideas, and in acceptance finding, a plan of action is developed to address the problem.

A third strategy, negotiation, has become a central component of managing group conflict and improving the dynamics of groups. For example, good leaders use "win-win" tactics that leave both sides of a conflict with an understanding that a decision was made in the best interest of both parties. Many other negotiation techniques have been found to be highly successful, and descriptions are available across the Internet.

<u>**4.4 B**</u>   **Promotes collaborative teaching and learning opportunities**

In Professional Learning Communities (PLCs), everyone views teaching and learning as a team effort. Classrooms do not operate as silos, but as interconnected units that support one another and that are mutually benefited from success. Administrators support collaboration by encouraging group planning, team teaching, and mentoring.

Teachers need to use a variety of instructional methods and techniques in the classroom. No two teachers will approach teaching the same objectives in the same way. For this reason, when teachers plan in a group, each member benefits from the input of the other members. In a planning group, seasoned or mentor teachers can help novice teachers plan a lesson to include both direct and guided, small-group instruction. Guided reading, for example, is a method of direct instruction to a small group of students who are all at the same reading level and need the same instructional strategy.

Team teaching can involve two teachers in the same classroom at the same time, both teaching the same subject. They can each be teaching small groups, or one teacher can instruct a group while the other helps individual students. Team teaching can also involve teachers of different subjects who integrate the learning objectives so they are reinforcing what the other teachers are doing in their classrooms. This type of instruction requires sufficient planning time, which may need to occur outside the regular school day. To facilitate planning, administrators in schools where team teaching takes place usually schedule the day so the teachers have their prep periods at the same time.

4.4 C Involves students as appropriate in school improvement teams and processes

Students don't only get knowledge; they can share knowledge as well. This group of stakeholders should have an active voice in key decisions. The older they are the more active should be their involvement. Students should be represented on the school improvement team, fundraising committees, and if age-appropriate, disciplinary boards. In many cases, it is most efficient to ensure student involvement by having a strong student council. This organization represents democratically elected individuals who can solicit buy-in from their peers. In addition, it provides an immediate pool of student leaders who can be called upon to provide feedback on important decisions. As an additional benefit, through their engagement, these students are developing important leadership skills.

Skill 4.5 Creates opportunities and a safe environment in which the staff can examine their own beliefs, values, and practices about teaching and learning

According to the Leadership Development National Excellence Collaborative, "collaborative leadership requires a new notion of power...the more power we share, the more power we have to use." This type of leadership is the skillful and mission-driven management of important relationships. It is the point at which organization and management come together. Additionally, collaborative leadership uses supportive and inclusive methods to ensure that all stakeholders affected by a decision are part of the change process. In particular, teachers and staff must feel that they are valued and that they will not be judged negatively for being open, honest, and flawed. Collaboration requires that individuals be able to present their perspectives and be honest about their biases. The group must then be willing to help each member work towards change.

Even if change does not occur, team members must be able to acknowledge that our biases play a role in our decisions and actions.

4.5 A   Provides a safe environment for teachers to express their beliefs and ideas

See Skill 4.5

4.5 B   Provides opportunities for teachers to take appropriate risks for improving teaching and learning

Trust is an important component in a learning community. If the principal respects each teacher and provides a safe environment for everyone to express their ideas and thoughts, much can be accomplished. This will only be reached in a non-judgmental environment that does not permit criticism of the ideas of others. Success in problem solving boosts teachers' confidence and makes them more willing to take risks. Therefore, the principal must provide opportunities for teachers to work together or independently to successfully solve instructional problems.

An atmosphere that frowns on *closed-mindedness* and rewards *openness* to new and different approaches and ideas is powerful in shaping teachers' attitudes. Some teachers will be used to administrators who are narrow-minded, judgmental, and critical. They may initially be skeptical of school leaders who say they encourage risk taking. By having a clear policy of risk-openness, the administrator can help even the most reluctant teacher search for research-based, cutting-edge practices to use in the classroom.

It is important to support and recognize teachers who use new techniques that are supported by research. This will encourage other educators to stay on top of new ideas in the field. By planning in teams, teachers can vet each others' ideas and provide useful feedback on how to avoid pitfalls while implementing something new and untested. The principal can minimize the fear of failure by implementing a non-threatening system for teachers to share their pros, cons, and lessons-learned. When teachers venture into uncharted territory, they should report back to the team in an appropriate amount of time. This will allow mistakes to be addressed and the technique can be put on hold or discarded if it is too resource-intensive or is not producing desirable results.

Skill 4.6   Provides ongoing feedback to teachers using data and evaluation methods that improve practice and student learning

See Skill 3.2

<u>**4.6 A**</u>   **Develops a process to provide feedback (e.g., co-teaching, peer coaching, classroom walkthroughs) to increase teacher effectiveness and student performance**

In addition to the strategies shared in Skill 4.4 B, administrators should realize that teacher effectiveness can be increased when they receive multiple methods of feedback. For instance, a school may utilize learning contracts for each student and his or her parents. This is a way to individualize instruction, make the student responsible for his or her own learning, and track progress on pre-established goals. It is also an effective way to monitor and address behavioral issues.

Interdisciplinary instruction enables teachers to teach objectives from several different courses at the same time. This approach can be used by teachers who teach all the subjects in a classroom. It can also be used by teachers who each teach a different subject, but who instruct the same groups of students. In this method, teachers can take the objectives from social studies, for example, and teach them along with language arts and math. This method allows peer-coaching to occur as the team of teachers provide feedback and help each other refine the instructional and assessment strategies.

In an effort to support teacher success, the state or district may provide assistance to new teachers and experienced teachers new to teaching in the state. The assistance of a peer teacher and a variety of induction activities enable teachers to receive assistance without the implied threat of evaluation. This open system allows teachers to seek help when they need it. By conducting informal walk-throughs, the administrator can conduct authentic assessments of each teacher. These snap-shots provide opportunities for every teacher to meet with the principal in one-on-one sessions. During the post-observation meeting, the principal can applaud strengths and the two professionals can collaboratively plan to address challenges that were observed.

<u>**4.6 B**</u>   **Participates in collaborative data analysis (e.g., evaluates student work, disaggregates test scores) to increase teacher effectiveness and student performance**

See Skill 1.1 B

Skill 4.7   **Guides and monitors individual teacher professional development plans and progress for continuous improvement of teaching and learning**

Just as the school must be guided by a plan with a vision and goals, each administrator and teacher should have a professional development plan to guide his or her practice. Often staff members are required to attend monthly or biweekly career and staff development meetings. This allows them to engage in professional development opportunities to learn effective instructional theories and practices. Typically, school budgets allow only minimal expenditures for staff professional development. Thus, administrators must climb a precarious slope when selecting developmental activities that can meet the individual and group needs of all teachers.

While most schools have career coordinators who direct students toward higher education or career choices, staff career coordination is usually the job of the administrative leader. It is also with the role of administration to provide leadership opportunities for staff to practice professional theory during staff meetings or in organized leadership seminars. In some school communities, entire departments create, for the staff, effective instructional strategies that are commonly and consistently used to promote student learning and achievement in their field. That is how future leaders and administrators are professionally grown.

Administrators must model a commitment to professional development by attending sessions to enhance their own practice. They should also engage in scholarly writing and work to publish articles in newsletters, journals, and books. Likewise, when administrators provide professional development that is inclusive of cultural identity and ethnic diversity, everyone wins by being presented with a global perspective. For teaching-certificate renewal, many school districts require each teacher and administrator to engage in a minimum of 150 hours of professional development. This benefits all stakeholders in the school community, so for administrators, facilitating professional development is both reflective and proactive.

COMPETENCY 005   RIGOROUS CURRICULUM AND INSTRUCTION

Skill 5.1   Develops a shared understanding of rigorous curriculum and standards-based instructional programs

A building administrator must help the learning community commit to a rigorous curriculum and relevant instructional program. High-level objectives have to meet or exceed state standards and be established for individual classes and the building as a whole. To attain success, careful planning must be used. The instructional team must determine and list the objectives and describe the type of work that would qualify as achieving these objectives. The team must consider students at various developmental-levels and create a program that meets the needs of students at each level.

The instructional objectives should reflect the level at which the students are operating in the cognitive, psychomotor, and/or affective domains. Therefore objectives should guide the selection of instructional resources and classroom activities, not vice versa. Objectives are aimed at general learning outcomes and must be stated in terms of observable student outcomes. For example, teachers may guide students in plotting coordinates on a graph. If the broad objective is "understands," then sub-objectives should describe what "understands" looks like. The chosen topic should be relevant to the students and should engage his or her interests and prior knowledge.

State and local standards or grade-level expectations are a safe starting point for determining objectives. Staff should work together to determine the lasting knowledge and abilities they want students to acquire. It is often helpful for teachers to plan by both subject area and grade level. The subject-area groups can work together to make sure that instruction focuses on the key areas that students will need to know from one grade to the next. Grade level teams can then focus on the key concepts that can be taught in an interdisciplinary manner.

5.1 A   Creates a culture supporting rigor and relevance in curriculum and instruction for all stakeholders

See Skill 5.1

5.1 B   Ensures school-wide practices and programs focus on a rigorous curriculum and standards based instruction

Administrators should provide teachers with ample resources to develop a toolkit of research-based instructional strategies, materials, and technologies. This will allow all teachers to develop instructions that are standards-based, rigorous, and relevant. In turn, this will encourage students to problem solve and think critically about subject content. When districts choose a curriculum, it is expected that students will master established benchmarks and standards of learning. Research on national and state standards indicates that all state assessments measure both national and state-level benchmarks and learning objectives. These apply to most subjects including science, foreign language, English/language arts, history, art, health, civics, economics, geography, physical education, mathematics, and social studies (Marzano & Kendall, 1996). Therefore, students need to master the mandated standards and perform well on state-required assessments. This can happen when administrators create a school-wide commitment to standards-based instruction.

5.1 C   Collaborates with teachers to develop and maintain an instructional program that ensures the standards-based curriculum is delivered

See Skill 5.1 and Skill 1.1 B

Skill 5.2   Works with teams, including teachers and other instructional staff, to analyze student work and monitor student progress

Students are at varying stages of development in any grade. Administrators and teachers must have knowledge of the developmental stages that children go through. Then they can have appropriate learning objectives and can monitor student progress in each domain. These domains include children's intellectual, social, emotional, physical, spiritual, and moral development. Teachers can plan in teams to create curricular outcomes and brainstorm about appropriate learning activities.

Also see Skill 2.3

Skill 5.3   Reviews and monitors curricular and instructional programs to ensure student needs are met

Program effectiveness is best measured through an ongoing and thorough evaluation plan. Program evaluation is the process of collecting and analyzing data to discover whether a design, development, or implementation is producing the desired outcomes. This may lead to changing or eliminating aspects of the program.

CIPP MODEL

The CIPP (Content Input Process Product) developed by Daniel Stufflebeam is a popular program evaluation model where, in a three-step process, information is provided for decisions; that obtained information is then delineated for collection, and provided to stakeholders.

Once the steps of the CIPP are completed, they must then correspond with four distinct types of evaluation: *content, input, process*, or *product* (Ornstein and Hunkins 1993). **Content evaluation** reviews the program environment and its met and unmet needs. Content evaluation provides baseline information related to the entire system of operation. **Input evaluation** provides information and determines how to utilize resources to attain the goals of the program. It focuses on whether the goals and objectives of the program are appropriate for the expected outcome or if the goals and objectives are stated appropriately. It also takes into account whether the resources to implement specific strategies are adequate, whether or not the strategies are appropriate to attain the goals, or if the time allotted is appropriate to meet the objectives set forth for the program.

In schools, *process evaluation* focuses on decisions regarding curriculum implementation. It is concerned with whether planned activities are being implemented, procedures are recorded as they occur, and monitoring is continuous to identify potential problems. Continuously identifying potential problems allows corrections to be made before or during the implementation of the program. For example, it might be necessary to establish special planning sessions or in-service workshops at specific grade levels to work on modifying strategies due to problems that have been uncovered. Process evaluation is also known as the piloting process prior to the actual implementation of a school-wide or district-wide program (Ornstein and Hunkins, 1993). Finally, *product evaluation* takes into account whether the final product or curriculum is accomplishing the goals or objectives and to what degree.

At this point decisions must be made regarding the continuation, termination, or modification of the program. Since the evaluation process is continuous, the evaluators may, at this point in the cycle, link specific actions back to other stages or make changes based on the data collected. The data obtained may indicate the need to delay full implementation of the program until corrections are made, or it may lead to the decision that the program is ready for large-scale implementation.

In summary, the main purpose of the evaluative process is to diagnose strengths and weaknesses, and to provide feedback to make appropriate decisions for programs and schools. The data collection for the evaluation process originates from a number of sources, including classroom observations, interviews and discussions with students, discussion with teachers and parents, testing and measurement data, information from pupil services or guidance services, and surveys of the school community.

5.3 A   Identifies student needs

There are many ways to evaluate student needs and to ensure that all goals are challenging yet achievable. First, school-wide achievement data should be analyzed. As a result of NCLB, most states and districts provide this information on a regular basis. In addition, special reports can be provided by state or district-level staff in the assessment or accountability office.

At the school level, administrators will need to solicit teacher support in obtaining classroom-wide student-need summaries. Teachers can check each student's reading level and prior subject area achievement. This information is usually in the cumulative file, located in the guidance office or the main office. This provides a basis for goal setting but shouldn't be the only method used. Depending on the subject area, other methods could be useful in determining if all goals are appropriate. They include:

- Basic skills tests
- Reading level evaluations
- Writing samples
- Interest surveys

In addition to these methods, informal observations should always be used. Finally, student levels of motivation must also be considered when addressing student needs.

5.3 B   **Develops plans to meet and monitor identified needs through appropriate curricular and instructional practices**

See Skill 5.3

Skill 5.4   **Provides coherent, effective guidance of rigorous curriculum and instruction**

See Skill 5.1 and Skill 5.1 B

5.4 A   **Engages actively in appropriate cross-disciplinary efforts to horizontally and vertically align curriculum and instruction**

The school leader will need to be an active part aligning the curriculum and instruction. The design team must specify each of the elements included in the design and develop a blueprint before implementation. The goals and objectives should be specific so that all stakeholders clearly understand what will be done and what behaviors are expected of learners. The next step is to identify the resources needed to attain curricular goals and objectives. Required material and human resources must be identified and secured. Materials may include textbooks, charts, maps, and other technology and equipment, such as projectors, computers, calculators, sports equipment, and microscopes. Human resources include administrators, teachers, volunteers, support staff, and others. Facilities are classrooms, gyms, athletic fields, cafeterias, and auditoriums. The subject matter, methods of organization, and activities, as well as the methods and instruments to evaluate the program, must be determined.

Curriculum Dimensions
The conceptual framework, the organization of the components of the curriculum, consists of two distinct dimensions: horizontal and vertical organization. *Horizontal organization* is a typical side-by-side course arrangement in which the concepts of one subject are presented relative to the concepts of another related subject. *Vertical organization* is concerned with longitudinal treatment of concepts within a subject across grade levels. The success of horizontal organization depends heavily on the collaboration of teachers of various disciplines at the same grade level, while vertical organization depends heavily on collaboration and planning among teachers of various grade levels.

The dimensions within the curriculum content must also be considered in curriculum design. Therefore, attention should be given to curriculum scope, sequence, integration, continuity, articulation, and balance.

- **Curriculum scope** refers to the breadth and depth of the curriculum content, learning activities, experiences, and topics.
- **Curriculum sequence** refers to the order of topics to be studied over time. The sequencing of the curriculum is usually organized from simple to complex topics; however, it can also emphasize chronological, whole-to-part, or prerequisite learning.
- **Curriculum integration** refers to linking the concepts, skills, and experiences in the subjects taught.
- **Curriculum continuity** deals with the smoothness of knowledge repetition from one grade level to another in specific subjects or areas of study.
- **Curriculum articulation** is the interrelationship within and among subjects both vertically and horizontally.
- **Curriculum balance** refers to the opportunities offered for the learners to master knowledge and apply it in their personal, social, and intellectual life pursuits.

Curriculum Design Principles

Curriculum content can be based on a number of different design principles. For example, *subject-centered* designs reflect the mental discipline approach to learning. The curriculum is organized according to essential knowledge that must be learned in the different subject areas.

The *discipline design* is based on the organization of content, which allows for in-depth understanding of the content and the application of meaning. It is used primarily in secondary schools to emphasize the organizational content inherent in disciplines such as science, math, and English. Using this approach, the emphasis is on experiencing the discipline as learning takes place.

Unlike the subject field, in which a subject is studied separately from other related subjects, in the *broad fields design*, related subjects are broadened into categories. For instance, in this design social studies encompasses history, geography, and civics, and physical science encompasses physics and chemistry. The intent of the broad fields design is to integrate the traditional subjects so the learner develops a broader understanding of the areas included.

The *process-centered design* addresses how students learn and apply learning processes to the subject matter. This design focuses on the student's thinking process and incorporates procedures for children to gain knowledge.

Skill 5.5 **Assures alignment of curriculum and instruction, student assessments, program evaluation methods, and professional development to content standards**

See Skill 5.5 A

5.5 A Analyzes school improvement documents to ensure these elements are met and linked together systematically

The annual Campus Improvement Plan (CIP) or School Improvement Plan (SIP) delineates the improvement targets for the school. The CIP lists the school's goals along with activities to accomplish the goals, a timeline for completion and the personnel assigned to monitor goal completion.

It has been said that everyone in a school is paying attention to what the principal is paying attention to. A principal must make sure that his/her words and actions match, and that there is a systematic link between the vision, goals, priorities, teaching and learning activities, assessments, evaluations, and professional development topics. Principals and teachers have limited time and energy. Every task undertaken requires asking, "Will this get me and my staff closer to our vision of what we want to accomplish for children?"

Skill 5.6 **Assists teachers with differentiated teaching strategies, curricular materials, educational technologies, and other resources**

Principals must support teachers who serve as facilitators of learning. The effective teacher takes care to select appropriate activities and classroom situations in which learning is optimized. *Instructional activities* and *classroom conditions* are manipulated in a manner that enhances group and individual learning opportunities. For example, the classroom teacher can plan group activities in which students cooperate, share ideas, and discuss topics. In addition to enhancing academic growth, cooperative learning can teach students to collaborate and share personal and cultural ideas and values. The principal can support these strategies by providing additional classroom staff or creating a school culture that engages parent or community volunteers.

Leadership is also an important ingredient in adopting and using technology. Without leadership from principals, teachers may be reluctant to introduce new methodologies into the learning process. They may resist integrating technology unless time is devoted to training and staff development.

Technology provides the greatest benefit when computers are placed in individual teachers' classrooms. This format maximizes both teacher and student access for a number of uses including remediation, drill-and-practice, and simulating real-world activities. Understanding the appropriate application of technology to specific curriculum and learning objectives is a key administrative skill. In an era of constructivist thinking in classrooms, where students take charge of their own learning, computer technology is perceived as an advantage to students' working independently, learning to think critically, and using computer technology as a productivity tool. Incorporating technology requires access and effective training for teachers to fully harness its power.

Skill 5.7   Ensures diverse needs of each student are addressed

5.7 A   Uses data to determine student needs

See Skill 5.3 A

5.7 B   Identifies and accesses resources that are available and needed by involving all stakeholders

The management of resources at a school is a difficult task. Principals are required to maintain budgets, identify funds from external sources, manage staffs that usually range from twenty to one hundred teachers (in addition to support personnel), and keep track of material resources such as office supplies, building materials, and instructional resources. How can a principal effectively do all this? First, every district has specific policies and procedures. The first thing a new principal should do is learn those procedures. Second, wherever a principal has discretion, attention and resources should be directed to achieving the school's mission and vision. Third, a principal can get the assistance of school personnel, parents, and other interested parties. Often, when schools have site-based management committees, those groups can represent various school needs that are affected by resource allocation.

After taking all of those issues into account, as resources are actually allocated, various procedures should be followed to record transactions. For example, as staff members are hired, principals can demonstrate alignment between the desired qualifications, the actual qualifications of the hired individual, the district policies, and the school's mission and vision. Doing such recording helps prevent concerns about decisions that are made.

The management of human, material, and financial resources requires careful documentation, clear policies, and effective communication. Resources of all types carry emotional and personal weight with school community members. Principals who forget about the political elements of running a school often find themselves having to repair relationships. Proactive principals, however, consider all political elements that might surface as they make decisions.

Skill 5.8   **Provides all students with preparation for and access to a challenging curriculum**

5.8 A   **Monitors instructional practices and student progress to assure that all students are prepared for and have access to a challenging curriculum**

See Skill 4.1 A and Skill 4.1 C

Skill 5.9   **Identifies and uses rigorous research- and data-based strategies and practices in ways that close opportunity and achievement gaps**

When designing strategies to close gaps in student achievement, good administrators stay on top of what is going on in the field. Research-oriented leaders regularly skim scholarly journals and research articles. Topics that seem promising are then read more carefully to glean and understand what is being proposed. In addition, the educator must ask questions such as:

- When was the article written?
- Who wrote it?
- What are the author's credentials?
- Are other writers/professionals writing or speaking about the same idea or approach?

INCORPORATING NEW IDEAS

Next, school leaders conduct their own literature search to see if they can find where the new theory or approach has been tested and what results have been found. In the case of a debate about a particular theory or practice, they take into account what they have found in their own experience. Just because it is written and published doesn't mean it is true, useful, or applicable to every educational situation. They also learn how to engage other stakeholders in vetting or evaluating the merits of a proposed strategy. Only after the idea passes all of these tests, will experienced leaders incorporate, rate, and evaluate it in their own practice.

5.9 A   **Leads staff in implementing strategies and monitoring effectiveness to close opportunity and achievement gaps**

See Skill 2.3 and Skill 1.1 B

Skill 5.10   **Conducts frequent classroom and school visits and observations to provide constructive and meaningful feedback to faculty and staff**

The principal must achieve work through and with others. Clearly defining work and outcomes is important. It is also important that feedback be provided regularly in ways that are meaningful and constructive. Written and oral daily or weekly progress reports serve as avenues to monitor the progress of work and to provide assistance when needed to meet established goals and objectives.

The progress of work should be monitored through a variety of means. Department chairpersons and grade level chairpersons are important partners in providing feedback to the principal. When work is assigned across grade and curriculum levels, the chairperson of the tasks should provide timely feedback to the principal. In determining how well progress is being made, the principal can use a variety of resources, such as norm-referenced and criterion-referenced tests, observations, report reviews, checklists, team reviews, and external evaluations to determine how the work of others is being performed and if it is being done in a timely manner.

Principals as instructional leaders must be present on the campus, regularly visiting classrooms and providing useful feedback to teachers. Principals can provide teachers with techniques and suggestions for improving practice; however, principals must do so while also encouraging and showing support to teachers. The bottom line is that educational leaders can only hold teachers accountable at the end of the year if they provide them feedback and support during the year. This is particularly true in a professional learning community where everyone works as a team for the common goal of maximizing student learning.

Skill 5.11   Develops a plan for frequent classroom and school visits to provide meaningful feedback

See Skill 5.10

COMPETENCY 006   ASSESSMENT AND ACCOUNTABILITY

Skill 6.1   Uses assessment and accountability systems to improve the quality of teaching and learning

See Skill 3.1, Skill 4.1 C, and Skill 4.2

6.1 A   Guides ongoing analyses of data about all students and subgroups to improve instructional programs

School administrators must implement appropriate assessments to measure individual student growth during the school year and from year to year. This should be ongoing rather than measuring student achievement at a single point in time. Analyzing these growth measures over time also helps to determine how student achievement is aligned with district or state standards. Teachers should also be able to determine if classroom instruction is challenging individual students appropriately.

Teachers must be encouraged to shift from assessment *of* learning to assessment *for* learning. Assessment for learning is a process in which evidence is used to determine where students are in their learning, where they need to go, and how best to get there. Assessment for learning is an ongoing process whereas assessment of learning is conducted at a single point in time for the purpose of summarizing the current status of student achievement.

Research shows that assessment is most effective when it:

- Is student-centered
- Is congruent with instructional objectives
- Is relevant
- Is comprehensive
- Is clear (in purpose, directions, expectations)
- Is objective and fair
- Simulates "end" behavior/product/performance
- Incites active responses
- Shows progress/development over time

Data-driven instruction is based on assessment data from various sources. Teachers should analyze state achievement scores, district and school benchmark scores, and formal and informal classroom assessments. This data provides valuable information about students' current understanding and learning. Teachers should use this data to determine if they are meeting established objectives, and re-plan or re-teach as necessary.

Skill 6.2   Analyzes multiple sources of data, including formative and summative assessments, to evaluate student learning, effective teaching, and program quality

Assessing and evaluating students are very important aspects of the teaching and learning process. Periodic testing collects data on learning outcomes based on established objectives. It also provides information at various stages in the learning process to determine future student needs such as periodic reviews, re-teaching, and enrichment. After the teacher and/or administrator reviews the data, learning activities are planned. At varying stages of the teaching and learning process, the intended outcome must be measured, the level of goal attainment established, and this continuous cycle of student evaluation proceeds.

EVALUATION AND MEASUREMENT OF STUDENT ACHIEVEMENT

Evaluation and measurement are often used interchangeably to imply the same process. However, while closely related, they should be differentiated. *Evaluation* is the process of making judgments regarding student performance, and *measurement* is the actual collection of data that are used to judge student performance. Evaluation is related to student performance when the focus is on how well a student carries out a given task or when student work is the focus of the measurement.

Three Types of Evaluation

The purpose of the student evaluation will determine the type of process to use. Diagnostic, formative, and summative evaluations are the three types most commonly used. *Diagnostic evaluation* is provided prior to instruction to identify problems, to place students in certain groups, and to make assignments that are appropriate to students' needs. While it is important to address the specific needs of students, teachers must be cautious of the ramifications of grouping children in homogeneous versus heterogeneous groups. It may appear to save time to group and work with children of similar abilities, yet it often fails to foster students' intellectual and social growth and development. In fact, it has been shown that children in mixed groups benefit from the diversity within the group.

Formative assessment/evaluation is used to obtain feedback during the instructional process. It informs teachers of the extent to which students are really learning the concepts and skills being taught. The information should lead to modifications in the teaching and learning process to address specific needs of the students before arriving at the end of the unit. Therefore, it must be done frequently, using the specific objectives stated for learning outcomes.

Summative assessment/evaluation is used to culminate a unit or series of lessons to arrive at a grade. Knowing the content studied and having the specific skills required to score well on tests are two different endeavors. Successful performances require not only learning content, but also following the format of the assessment. Often, standardized tests are considered to be summative assessments. Therefore, teachers must train students in test-taking skills such as following directions, managing time effectively, and giving special attention to the type of tests and the skills required.

Regardless of the type of assessment, educators must gather and analyze the information they yield to determine students' strengths and weaknesses. The problem areas uncovered should be discussed with students collectively and individually and with parents at parent-teacher conferences. Whether diagnostic, formative, or summative, the assessment and evaluation of student performance should be a continuous process.

Skill 6.3   **Interprets and communicates data about progress toward vision and goals to the school community and other stakeholders**

See Skill 2.3 and Skill 2.4

Skill 6.4   **Supports teachers in development of classroom assessments that are frequent, rigorous, and aligned with the school's curriculum, and provides meaningful feedback for instructional purposes**

See Skill 6.2

<u>6.4 A</u>   **Develops a plan that provides opportunities for collaboration and feedback about classroom assessments**

As highlighted in Skill 2.3, when schools operate as professional learning communities, work is completed in teams. A team of professionals develops lessons and likewise, a team works together to craft, pilot-test, revise, and finalize assessments. While many classroom-based assessments will only be worked on by an individual teacher, teams should be used for grade-wide and or subject-specific assessments. This is another strategy for ensuring that instruction covers what students need to know from one subject to the next and from one grade to the next.

DOMAIN III   MANAGING ORGANIZATIONAL SYSTEMS AND SAFETY

COMPETENCY 007   MANAGING OPERATIONAL SYSTEMS

Skill 7.1   Develops short term and long-range strategic plans and processes to improve the operational system

The term operational system refers to the resources, human and otherwise, and the operations/tasks that help an organization to operate. The more effective the operational system, the more effective the educational system it supports. For this reason administrators must verify that this system operates at its highest level. As with the academic functions, the operating components need to be supported by a team of individuals who are committed to a highly productive educational environment.

The most basic function is to help the organization operate in an efficient and cost-effective manner. When planning for the short-term, the administrator will need to appoint a skilled individual to manage the day-to-day functions of the operational department. This person will then lead a team of individuals who can procure, monitor, and allocate resources appropriately. Basic process documents will need to be developed and disseminated so that all employees are familiar with the proper way to do everything from ordering supplies to requesting service on equipment. The operational department can also be responsible for allocating such resources as audiovisual equipment, media resources and space, meeting rooms, teacher and staff offices, multipurpose rooms, classrooms, laboratories, cafeterias, playgrounds, indoor and outdoor space for physical education, and auxiliary spaces.

In the long-term, the administrator will need to plan for depreciation of assets. The team must also have a plan for replacing those items that are out-of-date or non-functioning. Technological investments also require significant long-term planning. Schools have scarce resources and limitless demands placed upon them. Technology is expensive and places tremendous demands on the budget. The proactive principal understands this and makes a plan to maximize available resources including relocation, renovation, and new construction. To maximize its benefits, the operational-system plan must be monitored. The department should report to the head administrator, superintendent, or principal on a regular basis. Data and usage trends should inform the discussion on how to revise the plan and improve the way the operational system functions.

Skill 7.2   Develops a process to ensure compliance with local, state, and federal physical plant safety regulations

To ensure that schools are safe, compliant, and comfortable, school leaders must be familiar with regulations at the federal, state, and local levels. While school districts and funding levels do play significant parts in the aesthetics of a school building, basic safety and comfort issues are the responsibilities of a school's administrative team. Various strategies can be put into place to promote satisfactory levels of building safety and efficiency.

First, a principal or designee—such as an assistant principal—should be responsible for knowing all the regulations that apply to the physical facilities. That individual is the contact-person for external and internal inquiries; in addition, he/she should make daily rounds to monitor the campus. To make the task systematic and consistent, a checklist should be created to identify key facilities and their statuses. Daily tasks might include visiting restrooms to ensure that everything is working properly and that students have clean, well-operating facilities. A checklist might also include examining the blacktop in the athletic areas to ensure that students are safe when running or playing outside.

Principals are also responsible for advocating for building comforts at the district and community levels. As one example, while not all districts can afford air conditioning, with a superintendent's approval, principals can make needs clear to local taxpayers. Although many school districts pay for utilities, school building leaders can still examine utility usage for efficiency. Problems may be noted in terms of air drafts, heating duct problems, and plumbing.

Finally, school leaders should report to the district's buildings' manager if there are problems that pose safety or privacy concerns. For example, if a bathroom stall door does not work properly, either a building-level custodian must fix it, or if the building-level resources are not available a district support staff member should fix it. The same is true for issues of safety, such as ceiling panels that are about to fall down in a classroom.

Skill 7.3 Facilitates communication and provides for data systems that ensure the timely exchange of information

Electronic communications have helped to reduce logistical barriers to timely communication. For these strategies to be as effective as possible, the school or school system must create a system that encourages using these technologies. For instance, by providing internet access in all classrooms, the school can ensure that teachers can receive emails and access the district or school intranet during the school day or while they are on break. To minimize communication barriers, stakeholders must feel that they are involved in a system that encourages openness, honesty, timeliness, and trustworthiness. There is a delicate balance that must be maintained. While some information must be shared on a very limited basis and will take time to be vetted appropriately, other news should be delivered as soon as possible to as many people as possible.

For appropriate communication flow, the school must adopt and utilize a formal system for processing new information, determining how and when the information will be presented, and then sharing it appropriately. For some districts or schools, the sharing phase may rely on posting the information on their main website or sending out alerts by email, text message, or mass calling. Other schools may have to post quick highlights on a bulletin board near school entrances. In that way, even if they do not have access to the internet or emails, parents can quickly stay in-the-loop. Posting a brief note on the school marquis is another strategy to remind parents to check their students' folders for more information.

Skill 7.4   Acquires equipment and technology and monitors its maintenance and appropriate use

Human resources are made even more effective when they have the necessary equipment and technology to support their efforts. The principal should have a technology coordinator to whom he or she can delegate necessary responsibilities. Significant energies must be devoted to researching, comparing, and acquiring items. Likewise, time must be spent in sharing the appropriate use policy and in making sure that all resources are maintained in a way that maximizes their life span.

Technology is integral to modern instruction and learning. Determining how best to incorporate computer technology into the curriculum is a time-consuming process. In fact, the appropriate design and integration of computer technology into a school's curriculum is a major undertaking.

Computers can only be significant in the teaching and learning process when the advantages and applications are carefully thought out and implemented. Traditional uses of computers in classrooms, such as drill and practice, games, and remediation under-use the capabilities of computers and software applications, which can be a versatile teaching tool with infinite potential. Computer technology can be used to support students in analysis, creative thinking, and problem solving. Specifically, information management, writing, and mathematical concepts can all be taught using the computer.

Video also has a powerful potential for education (Maurer & Davidson, 1998). Video formats have the potential for being the most creative educational applications developed thus far (Picciano, 1998). Moving images have an advantage over still visuals in the teaching and learning process. Video can be used in the learning environment for both affective and cognitive learning. Video technology comes in a variety of formats. DVD, videodisc, VHS videocassette, videocassette (8 millimeter), and compact discs are common media being used in the instructional process today.

Each of these formats presents advantages and disadvantages in the instructional environment. Video technology can be used to analyze human interactions, mastery of skills through repeated observations, and the shaping of attitudes (Heinich, Molenda, Russell, & Smaldino, 1996). However, in the classroom, it can promote inactive learning. Teachers need to ensure that their use of video technology in the classroom is appropriated for deep learning.

7.4 A   Develops a plan for acquisition and maintenance of equipment and technology

See Skill 7.4

7.4 B   Creates an appropriate use policy and monitors compliance

The Appropriate Use Policy is also known as a Fair Use Policy or Acceptable Use Policy (AUP). This document outlines the way in which the school's technology can be used. It must be clear and concise so that all users can understand the rules they must follow. Many school systems require that before they are allowed to access the services, users agree to an AUP or Terms of Service document. The AUP should clearly outline the consequences of violating the rules and these policies must be monitored and enforced.

For instance when users damage equipment, they may be barred from using any other equipment in the future. It may also be appropriate for their user accounts to be suspended or terminated. In extreme circumstances, legal actions should be taken. The technology coordinator should be well trained in internet security and in the most recent strategies to keep students safe while using technology and the internet in particular.

COMPETENCY 008   ALIGNING AND OBTAINING FISCAL AND HUMAN RESOURCES

Skill 8.1   Allocates funds based on student needs within the framework of local, state, and federal regulations

Administrators are required to understand and implement the processes of planning, developing, implementing, and evaluating a district budget. The district budget is provided by the legislature and is dispensed according to the number of students in school buildings on October 1 of each school year. The budget includes a specific allocation for regular education students and greater amounts for special education and bilingual students. The budget for students with special needs includes additional monies for instructional aides and special Individual Education Plan (IEP) provisions that students may require. The bilingual budgets are also allocated to provide for instructional assistants and additional resource materials for students.

Building a school budget based on the monies distributed by a district is difficult. A proactive administrator creates a spreadsheet showing budget allocations for each department over a three-year span. Showing the trends and allocation of monies can indicate where shifts of funding need to occur to maximize program outputs for both staff and students. Administrators bring budget issues to the building leadership teams, which vote to accept or reallocate funding among the various departments and/or programs.

Since monies are quite tight for schools these days, budgets are particularly important for schools struggling to implement basic, core academic programs and provide intervention programs for struggling students. Most school budgets are designed to cover the basics; thus, an administrator must cover these costs before any extra monies can be given to programs or additional staffing. The majority of a school's budget goes to staffing and the rest is used to finance additional areas voted on by the building leadership team.

Within the budget are additional dollars given to special education programs and bilingual programs. This additional money goes toward providing specialized instructional assistants who can support student learning as interpreters or in other duties as assigned. The administrator is truly a transformational leader and constructive accountant if he or she can creatively use a budget to address the majority of instructional and facilitator concerns in a building.

8.1 A   Develops and monitors a budget process that involves appropriate stakeholders

To provide appropriate fiscal management for the economic and efficient operation of the school, school administrators must be familiar with basic accounting principles. Accounting is the process of recording, presenting, summarizing, and interpreting financial data. The school leader must be able to collect and track all the funds that are used by the school on a day-to-day basis. To do this he or she must have a budget committee who meets and reports on a regular basis. Together with the principal, these individuals are responsible for reviewing income, expenses, and requests for purchases.

PRINCIPLES OF SCHOOL ACCOUNTING

General principles of school cost accounting use an accrual rather than a cash basis accounting system. Using the accrual basis of accounting, financial transactions of the school must be recorded as revenues or expenditures at the time the transaction occurs, and there should never be cash exchanged for goods or services. Revenues earned at the time of the transaction become assets, and expenditures become liabilities, regardless of when the cash receipt or reimbursement occurs. In this system of accounting, assets are inventory, investments, accounts receivables, building, and fixed equipment, furniture, motor vehicles, etc.; while liabilities are salaries, benefits, accounts payable, construction contracts, etc. Unlike private enterprises for profit where there is owners' equity, schools are owned by the taxpayers. Therefore, balances are known as fund equity, which include reserves, retained earnings, and contributed capital.

Rules for Internal Funds

Schools must adhere to specific rules governing their internal funds as prescribed by state board rules. All school organizations must be accountable for receipts and expenditures of funds obtained from the public. Additionally, sound business practices are expected for all financial transactions of the school. For example, in an effort to raise money to benefit programs of the school, fundraising activities should not conflict with the programs administered by the school board.

All purchases using internal funds must be authorized by the principal or designee and require the district's preapproved, serially numbered receipt forms to record any cash received and to record the accounting transaction. Each school must have a bank checking account, and each monthly statement must be reconciled as soon as it is received. Each account should have two authorized check signers, one being the principal. The principal should never pre-sign checks, under any circumstances. Monthly written financial reports must be created for the purpose of school decision making, and annual reports must be created for the district's annual financial statement.

The sponsors of classes, clubs, or departmental student activities (such as athletic events, musical groups, math club, etc.) are responsible for providing the financial documents and records to the principal or designee. The collection received must be deposited in the school internal fund in the respective classified account. All disbursements by the club or organization must be made by check from internal funds. A financial report must then be filed with the principal's office at the close of each fundraising activity.

Continuous Auditing

Records and documents of school financial transactions for its internal fund and accounts must be examined periodically through the auditing process. Whether internal or external, audits provide an adequate safeguard to preserve the property of the public school system. This process provides evidence of the propriety of completed transactions; it determines whether all transactions have been accurately recorded in the appropriate accounts, and whether the statements have been drawn from the accounts.

Good auditing reviews are the result of excellent accounting practices. Drake and Roe (1994) define the accounting cycle as continuous and inclusive of documenting, analyzing, recording, and summarizing financial information. Documenting means recording all financial transactions including the authority or initiator of the transaction, ensuring that the debt incurred is within the limit of allotment, that every financial transaction is identified with a unit or fund, and that each fund is restrictive and limited in use. The process of analyzing requires that each transaction is classified into debits or credits, and that each debit or credit is referenced to a specific account under the affected fund. It also requires a clear understanding of how a debit or credit affects the balance in an account, and that budgetary accounts are restricted in purpose and amount of expenditure. The recording and summarizing processes require that all transactions of a fund or account be recorded and that summaries be provided to allow comparisons and analyses of the changes that are taking place within the budget.

Managing the Budget

Future resources for education are planned through student enrollment forecasts. From the appropriated funds, the district builds its budget. At this point, the budget becomes an important device for translating the educational plan into a financial plan. The budget is, in effect, the translation of prioritized educational needs into a financial plan, which is interpreted for the public in such a way that when it is formally adopted, it expresses the kind of educational program the community is willing to support financially and morally for a one-year period (Drake and Roe, 1994).

The budget must be managed through a financial system of accounting. Sources of revenue can be federal, state, or local funds. Expenditures, on the other hand, are categorized by dimensions, which include funds or account groups, objects, functions, facilities, projects, and reporting. The funds or account groups are accounting entities with a self-balancing set of accounts that supports specific school activities to attain specific objectives. Therefore, funds or accounts can only be used for specified purposes.

A predetermined local formula allows expenditures from the general fund to be used for the day-to-day operations of schools. Additionally, a school may have an activity account and a school internal account. The activity account is derived from class fees, athletic contests, and events, plays, yearly photos, and other special programs. While the proceeds belong to the school, they must be used for students' learning benefits such as award ribbons, trophies, and the like. These proceeds must be identified, and accounted for, in the same manner as any other funds of the school.

Zero-based budgeting is a form of accounting in which all expenditures must be justified in each new period. This is in contrast to only justifying the amounts requested that are in excess of the funding levels of the previous period.

Skill 8.2 Implements effective strategies to recruit and retain highly qualified personnel

The educational leader of a school must possess a number of competencies. The most time-consuming involves human resource management and development. Educational leaders must know and understand human relations since schools are labor-intensive and personnel uses 80 to 90 percent of a school's budget. Over time, the personnel management roles of school administrators have expanded. Therefore, understanding the many aspects of personnel management is essential in creating and maintaining a successful and efficient school organization.

The selection of instructional and non-instructional personnel is often considered the most important aspect of the principal's position. It is through people that the principal is able to achieve the mission of the school; therefore he or she should lead the staff in a collegial environment. The principal should convey that school personnel are of greatest importance, and do everything in his or her power to provide the best possible working conditions. Once they are empowered, the personnel will subsequently be empowered to do what is best for the students.

PLANNING, RECRUITMENT, AND INTERVIEWING

In selecting instructional personnel, the principal has many responsibilities. Planning, recruitment, and selection are essential aspects of securing personnel. Planning requires the principal to look at the current staff and plan for future short-term and long-term needs. Using site-based management, the principal involves current personnel in developing and revising the personnel plan for the school. During this process, consideration must be given to current staff, students, parents, the community, school district, and state and federal rules and regulations. Facilities, equipment, and other factors must be reviewed at this time also.

Planning must be comprehensive, take place well in advance of the need, and allow sufficient time to prepare papers and get approval through the district system. The principal must know the process used in the school district to select personnel, including how assignments are determined and the impact of the collective negotiation contract (if there is one in the district). The plan must also provide for emergencies such as unexpected promotions, illnesses, resignations, and terminations.

Once the plan is complete, recruitment can begin; this is a critical component of successful human resource management. First, the principal must understand the procedure in his or her district. Recruitment must occur early, whether the principal has control of the entire process and uses a selection committee or the district does the recruiting and has to give approval to fill the positions. Second, the administrator must identify sources for qualified applicants with staff diversity factoring into the hiring mix. College and university career offices, schools of education, and career fairs at the state and local levels are among popular recruitment options. Dialogue with colleagues and current school staff also offer opportunities to recruit new employees.

The Selection Process
The selection process involves screening the paperwork, interviewing candidates, and checking references. The selection committee must understand the confidential nature of applicant information and must be charged with maintaining the integrity of the process. Using a job-related matrix for the position, each applicant's papers are evaluated against the criteria. Unqualified applicants are removed from the candidate pool. Although certification in the field is one of the most crucial factors to consider, the quality of the application is also judged for training competencies, job stability, comprehensiveness, grammar, and neatness.

Qualified applicants are then interviewed, the most time-consuming phase of personnel selection. After candidates are notified of the time and location for the interview, the committee determines questions to be asked and criteria for judging the responses. Each candidate for a position must be asked the same questions and judged by the same criteria. The committee then submits to the principal the names of the most qualified applicants, usually three to five individuals.

The principal reviews the work of the committee, interviews the potential employees, and conducts reference checks. Notification is sent to candidates informing them of their selection or non-selection. Another good strategy is to visit the person's current or most recent place of employment. Principals often contact the institutions that trained the potential employee to obtain professional judgments about the candidate. Retrieving fingerprint records ensures that known criminals are not employed. Last, the principal recommends to the superintendent the person who should be employed.

Finally, with No Child Left Behind and its emphasis on "highly qualified teachers," principals have to abide by state and federal laws regarding licensure/certification and degrees. For example, all secondary subject-area teachers must have a degree (or demonstrate extensive competency, usually through a very rigorous exam) in the subjects they will be teaching.

Compensation and Reward Systems
A compensation and reward system is required in any organization. A compensation program attracts, maintains, and motivates good employees. It also creates incentives for continual growth and maintains budgetary control in school districts (Webb, Greer, Montello, and Norton, 1996). Merit pay, paid leave, child care, cost-of-living increases, salary schedules, extracurricular stipends, early retirement plans, tax-sheltered annuities, and medical plans are types of compensation and rewards. In addition, Social

Security benefits, retirement plans, severance pay, transportation allowances, and leaves of various types (sick, annual, sabbatical, religious, military, and professional) are included. Supply and demand often determine the package available to employees. Many districts are currently experimenting with pay-for-performance plans, where bonuses are given to teachers who increase their students' test scores. This has been highly controversial, because statistical models to determine teachers' impact on students' test scores is complicated and imprecise.

INDUCTION PROCESS

The induction process is another important component of a school district's offerings. Newly hired teachers receive assistance because they usually need more support than experienced teachers. The first part of the induction process is orientation to introduce the procedures, paperwork required, teaching and learning expectations, rules, and other aspects of the school culture. In some systems the district conducts the orientation, with the school providing additional orientation for those factors unique to the school. The socialization process is another critical facet, which can determine how well new personnel adapt and contribute to the teaching/learning community. The induction process typically ranges from ninety days to a full school year. The best approach lasts a year and pairs a neophyte teacher with a mentor who teaches the same grade level and subjects.

Administrators are responsible for recruiting, selecting, and inducting effective school personnel. The significance of this responsibility can be seen in the current national research that shows that of all high school graduates, only about 72 percent enrolled as freshmen in college. The dropout rate for high school students is estimated to be around 20-30 percent.

Remediation of high school graduates in two- and four-year colleges is estimated to affect almost 30 percent of incoming freshmen. Students may have impressive graduation portfolios that suggest a correlation between academic performance and college preparedness, but the reality is that a greater percentage of students are being underserved by schools. To combat these statistics, administrators are expected to recruit the best and brightest teachers.

The cost of hiring the best teachers is directly translated into high graduation rates and lower dropout rates for students who have demonstrated proficiency and knowledge acquisition during their high school career. With current federal mandates of the No Child Left Behind Act and adequate yearly progress (AYP) hiring requirements, administrators must hire according to legislative expectations. The law requires that newly hired teachers possess the credentials and endorsements of being certified, highly qualified, or experienced.

EVALUATING APPLICANTS

The administrative interview team consists of an administrator who evaluates the department in which personnel are being sought, along with certified and classified staff who has undergone interview training according to union guidelines and a parent volunteer who can represent the parent voice in the process. The team must review the paperwork for all applications using both subjective and objective methods of evaluation. The objective component includes a list of yes-and-no questions that are used to evaluate the potential of candidates who will eventually be offered an interview.

The subjective part of the application is used to evaluate the quality of the applicants' written responses to a series of questions. The corresponding score range is 1-5 (with one being the lowest and 5 the highest). It is the administrator's job to compile the quantitative data to determine the top three to five candidates to be interviewed. The interviews are typically twenty to thirty minutes long and extend beyond the school day and the contractual obligations of the teachers. Parent volunteers may take off from work or revise their afternoon schedules to accommodate the interview team.

The recruitment process is directed by district advertisement, school advertisement, and word of mouth. Recommendations are sought within the district and schools where college interns may be professionally developed in subject content areas. Administrators provide constant monitoring and evaluation of college interns, so interns' preparation and instructional abilities have been observed and documented.

Skill 8.3   Assigns personnel to address student needs, legal requirements and equity goals

The administrator of any school is charged with ensuring that the programs, services, and personnel are in place to meet the needs of all students in the school. This means ensuring that the teachers are in place for all grade levels, or in the case of junior high and high schools, teachers are in place for all subjects. It is also the responsibility of the administrator to ensure that the teachers have the proper training and are suited to these grade levels and subjects.

PROGRAMS

In addition to ensuring that programs are in place to meet the needs of the students who are struggling, there should also be programs in place to meet the needs of gifted and talented students. In most cases, schools do not have the budget needed to hire special teachers, nor should these students be segregated from their peers. Therefore, classroom teachers should provide challenging experiences and activities that meet the learning objectives and yet also meet the needs of students who are exceeding the objectives.

Special education for struggling students involves having the personnel in place to meet their specific needs. In classrooms, teachers should provide extra support for these students, but there should also be personnel who can pull them out of class to provide extra instruction in the areas in which they are experiencing difficulty. Testing procedures should also be in place so teachers can determine exactly what the problems are and how best to address them. In most schools, this testing is done by educational psychologists and reading specialists who come to the school on a regular basis and meet with students, teachers, and parents. These ancillary services also include mental health workers, home-school liaison personnel, health professionals, and the police who come to the school to meet with students and help them through times of difficulty.

ROLE OF THE PRINCIPAL

The role of the principal has indeed changed over the past ten years. Previously, principals functioned like the manager of the school building; they made sure that everything was working together according to specification. Duties included ensuring that activities were safe and cost effective; that all students had places to go during the day; that students were behaving properly; and that teachers had the resources they needed to teach.

Recently, there has been a shift to thinking of principals as instructional leaders. They are expected to be thoroughly aware of each classroom, the instructional styles of each teacher, and the learning outcomes of all students. They are held responsible for the quality of instruction and the depth of learning at their schools.

With this shift of responsibilities, though, comes a dilemma for most school leaders: should they focus on instruction at the expense of all other areas they know to be effective in the development of student growth, or should they concentrate on the refinement of a positive school culture? More challenging still, do they try to balance both demands—which takes much more time, money, and effort?

Most principals would argue that both are necessary, and that cost should not be a factor. They realize that students, their families, and teachers need to see that all students' needs are met on a variety of levels. Schools are ideal places to provide various athletic, creative, and intellectual activities. Furthermore, these activities provide schools with a greater sense of community.

How do principals balance those two disparate roles, as well as facilitate the development, implementation, evaluation, and refinement of student services and activities to fulfill academic, developmental, social, and cultural needs? First, principals must focus on the school's mission. Most schools' mission statements go beyond test scores and student achievement. For example, a school that says that its mission is to prepare students to succeed in a changing world will ultimately acknowledge that achievement is important. However, such a school will also offer students opportunities to succeed socially, physically, and creatively. As school needs are identified in order to reach those broad goals, principals can help select faculty to participate; they can also set aside money. As they allocate school resources—money, personnel, time, and space—they must be careful to ensure that students are treated fairly and equally. In this day and age, directing significant resources to the football team—and few resources to the chess team—may be seen as highly unfair.

STUDENT SERVICES

In addition to activities, principals must ensure that student services are nimble and responsive to needs that may arise at random times. For example, a highly bureaucratic student services office may not respond quickly when emergencies arise and students—en masse—need counseling. Such offices also need to pay close attention to the requests of parents. Principals can help to facilitate this by instituting planning sessions and regular meetings to review policies, procedures, and school goals. Student services personnel should play critical roles throughout the campus so that they address the concerns and needs of teachers as well as students when they are in academic and athletic environments.

Skill 8.4   Conducts personnel evaluations that enhance professional practice in accordance with local, state, and federal policies

Appraisal of personnel is a significant part of a principal's responsibility. Most districts use district-wide criteria developed through a diverse committee of representatives from the school community. These criteria provide the principal with objective and reliable methods of appraising staff. Teachers are also aware of the criteria and understand how they are used in evaluations. Gossip, unsigned notes, and other such techniques are deemed unreliable and should not be used.

In evaluating building-level staff, principals must know the district's criteria. For many teacher evaluations, states require performance-based assessments; therefore, the principal must tie performance to student learning. If the principal needs to acquire additional information on the development and implementation of the appraisal process, he or she can contact district or state officials, university professors, professional organizations, or consultants.

In an effort to support teacher success, the state or district may provide assistance to new teachers and experienced teachers new to teaching in the state. The assistance of a peer teacher and a variety of induction activities enable teachers to receive assistance without the implied threat of evaluation. This open system allows teachers to seek help when they need it.

When the evaluation process is conducted properly, teachers grow professionally and students benefit from increasingly effective instruction. Teachers should set professional development goals based on weak areas and receive recognition for areas of strength. The processes for gathering the data used to rate teachers should also be published and discussed. Most often, there are formal, planned classroom observations, as well as informal walk-throughs and other informal methods for viewing a teacher's work.

Teacher performance ratings should be directly tied to student achievement, so student achievement data should be included in determining appraisal scores. The driving motto should be that teaching has not happened unless students have learned!

Teachers should be given clear feedback about whether their performance is satisfying the criteria of the appraisal instrument. Delivering this feedback to the teacher in a face-to-face conference allows the appraiser to establish a dialogue with the teacher about instructional practices. Very few professionals, including teachers, change simply because someone talks to them. To change behavior, administrators must change the thinking behind the behavior. This can be achieved by asking questions that cause teachers to reflect on their own practices.

As a principal, your goal is to improve your staff so that student achievement will be optimized. You will encounter underperforming teachers who are in need of assistance. With these individuals, agree on two or three improvement goals and concentrate on making progress in these areas before moving on to other areas of need. Document the improvement plan and any progress, or lack of progress, toward the selected goals. Poorly trained teachers need to observe excellent role models, so allow release time for teachers to observe in other classrooms. Conferencing with the mentee after the observation will assist them in applying what they observed in their own classroom. When a teacher is working through an improvement plan, the principal should make more frequent visits to the classroom and look for signs of improvement. Document every visit and intervention. Ineffective teachers can improve with a principal's support, training, and mentoring.

The appraisal process is also a way to provide recognition for outstanding teachers. When a teacher's performance is highly rated, this provides encouragement to continue instructional practices that benefit students. Appraisal systems allow for the structured feedback that teachers need to improve instruction and grow professionally.

Also see Skill 4.6 A

Skill 8.5   Seeks additional resources needed to accomplish the vision

It is rare for municipal allotments to cover all the expenses incurred by the school or district. Superintendents and principals are more frequently using grant-writing skills to secure external funds for their organizations. To provide the necessary resources, principals must be creative in other ways as well. Fundraising efforts engage the community, volunteer corps help reduce personnel costs, and waste-reduction efforts all go a long way.

COMPETENCY 009   PROTECTING THE WELFARE AND SAFETY OF STUDENTS AND STAFF

Skill 9.1   Ensures a safe environment by proactively addressing challenges to the physical and emotional safety and security of students and staff

Schools must be safe places for students to learn and teachers to work. When emergencies occur, clear procedures must be in place to ensure that the school community responds in an orderly fashion. The administration must ensure that safety is a priority by first keeping everything in operable condition. Any broken item that could pose a safety risk should be dealt with. Furniture that gets in the way of door openings must be moved. All windows and doors should be completely operable and able to be opened quickly in an emergency. Air conditioners, heaters, gas systems, plumbing, and electricity must all be turned off easily and quickly if the need arises. This last point is a particular concern for many schools. Often, a specific custodian knows how to complete all safety procedures. However, if that individual is not on campus at a particular time, other individuals must know how to operate such equipment.

In planning for evacuation, routes should be drawn so that each hallway has the least possible number of students walking through, with no student having to walk too far. In other words, usually the quickest route out of a building may clog a hallway, thereby making the route much slower. However, it would also be unwise to have a whole classroom full of students walk a long way to avoid a particular hallway because they might still be in a potentially dangerous location. Often, fire departments or safety consultants can assist in designing safe, well-thought-out evacuation plans.

The opposite of an evacuation plan would be a lock-down plan. A lock-down plan would consist of various rules and procedures for getting or keeping all students in a secure location such as a classroom. The problem with a lock-down is often that communication suffers. Many schools around the country are now insisting that school personnel check their e-mail accounts as soon as a lock-down occurs, because e-mail can be a very efficient way to communicate with many people quickly. Whatever the plan, it is crucial that all stakeholders know what to do. Administrators, teachers, parents, teachers, and other stakeholders must be informed of the procedures that will be taken in the event that an emergency occurs.

9.1 A   Develops and implements a plan that involves appropriate stakeholders to ensure a safe teaching and learning environment

To ensure student and personnel safety, various levels of planning must be implemented. Plans must exist for ensuring safety in a variety of situations. Local natural disasters must be accounted for, as should plans for ensuring safety when, for example, the police are searching for a loose criminal in the surrounding neighborhood. Many schools may even have to consider safety plans for local terrorist attacks, particularly if the school is located near a busy or popular area. Plans should include methods for getting students in a safe area, as well as communication among staff members and between administrative personnel and parents or media. An effective strategy involves creating a safety committee. Comprised of a representative from each stakeholder group, the individuals would provide feedback to the committee and disseminate information to his or her constituents.

Fire drills tend to become routine for most staff and students, typically because they have never experienced a fire in the building. However, good administrators find creative ways to ensure that all staff members and students know the procedures. Directions should also be posted all over campus and be mailed home to parents annually.

When disasters or safety concerns occur, school leaders must behave like flight attendants, be calm and collected, but decisive and clear. During an emergency, when the leadership gives clear instructions, is wise in what information is shared and what is withheld, and acts decisively, the outcome is much better. After events that compromise safety, principals must do a few things. First, they must immediately debrief the district administrators, local police, staff, parents, students, and sometimes the media. Second, they must sit with other staff members and discuss the crisis response. From that discussion, the team can then make informed modifications to the plans.

New plans must then be communicated to all stakeholders. If there are no situations that require emergency plans to be implemented, the leader must still take the time to review what has been set in place. Along with the safety committee, he or she should walk through the plan, make sure that no new situations will prevent it from being implemented, and then work to remind everyone about the plan.

9.1 B   Conducts ongoing reviews of the plan

See Skill 9.1 A

Skill 9.2   Advocates for and oversees counseling and health referral systems that support student learning and welfare

Today's school leaders recognize that students learn best when they feel well, having coping skills to handle emotional issues, and know that the school cares for their well being. Principals should hire specific individuals or designate an office where students can be referred. When students need more care than can be delivered in house, the principal and the physical/mental health care staff must be cognizant of the policy set by the school system. Often, the system has its own counselors or has developed a relationship with external providers. By following the protocol, the school can refer students who are in need of more in depth health care or counseling services.

9.2 A   Identifies counseling and health needs of students to support student learning and welfare

The principal must work with his or her team to make sure the system operates quickly and is flexible. For example, a highly bureaucratic student services office may not respond quickly when emergencies arise and students—en masse—need counseling. Such offices also need to pay close attention to the requests of parents. Principals can help to assure this by instituting planning sessions and regular meetings to review policies, procedures, and school goals. The health care and counseling staff should be visible throughout the campus. By building rapport with parents, teachers, and students, health care staff members are more likely to learn about students who need their services but might go unnoticed or un-referred.

9.2 B   Takes steps to meet the identified needs

See Skill 9.2 and Skill 9.2 A

Skill 9.3   Involves teachers, students, and parents in developing, implementing, and monitoring guidelines and norms of behavior

Some causes of student misbehavior in school are desire for attention, need for power, lack of self-confidence, and wanting revenge. When students do not behave and medical reasons are identified, medication can often correct the issues. Regardless of the reason, when students have negative attitudes toward school, learning, and/or authority, there will be problems. To correct the problems, students must be held accountable for their behavior and the school must help them learn appropriate actions.

At the beginning of the school year, or preferably over the summer, administrators should convene a behavioral committee of staff, parents, and students. This group would be charged with learning the district's code of conduct and with adding elements that are important for the culture of their school. The adopted school code of conduct will then serve as the foundation for the behavioral expectations and corrective actions for the school year.

As the school year progresses, teachers can identify students with persistent behavioral challenges. Then each staff member can choose a student they will mentor throughout the year. This is all done without the students' knowledge. The staff members then try to make contact with the students at one or two points during the day to talk to them, ask them how their day is going, or to ask if they need any help. Research has shown that in schools where this method has been tried, behavioral problems were cut in half by the middle of the school year.

When dealing with young children, it is important to deal with only one or two behaviors at a time. Often the problem is that young children do not have the skills to solve their immediate problems and they lash out with behaviors that are unacceptable. When educators address the behaviors by also teaching problem-solving skills, students learn how to deal with issues in a proactive and independent manner.

To address behavioral issues, educators must let students know that they care about them. The school must be a safe and caring place where students feel protected. In most cases parents are important team members who work with educators for the best interest of the child. Unfortunately, in some instances parents are the cause of the problem and the school will need to act in the best interest of the child. For instance, teachers may notice bruises on a child and will learn that his or her parent attempted to deal with misbehavior by using disciplinary methods that cannot be condoned or ignored. In these cases, outside agencies, such as the police and a social service agency, will have to be involved.

Skill 9.4   Develops with appropriate stakeholders a comprehensive safety and security plan

See Skill 9.1 A

9.4 A   Conducts ongoing reviews of the plan

See Skill 9.1 A

Skill 9.5   Identifies key emergency support personnel in and outside of the school

As discussed in Skills 9.1 through 9.4, to maintain safety with the school, administrators will need to enlist the support of numerous organizations and individuals both internally and externally. Internally the school will count on the safety committee and the health care staff or office. The administration should provide an organizational chart with names, phone numbers, and email addresses. While the detailed document might only be distributed to staff members, parents should also be provided with a simplified list of contacts.

Staff members should also receive a list of district-level emergency support personnel. The more comprehensive list should be stored in the main office and it should include cellular phone numbers and may even have home numbers to reach pertinent officials in the event of an emergency that is large in scale or that presents imminent danger. Typically this information is also maintained electronically in a password-protected environment such as on the school district's intranet site.

School leaders will also need to understand the chain of command to be followed in emergency situations. Homeland security and emergency preparedness requirements have mandated that educational bodies establish guidelines for who should be contacted at each level of the system. For instance the principal would share information with his or her area superintendent who then talks with the superintendent. The superintendent and his or her cabinet-level staff may then be the ones who share information with the state department of education, the media, and the federal homeland security officers.

9.5 A   Identifies and documents key emergency support personnel in and outside of the school

See Skill 9.5

9.5 B   Communicates the information about key emergency support and school personnel to appropriate parties

See Skill 9.5

Skill 9.6   Communicates with staff, students, and parents on a regular basis to discuss safety expectations

See Skill 9.1, Skill 9.1 A, and Skill 9.3

9.6 A   Documents communication of safety expectations to staff, students, and parents

When information is shared with members of the school community, administrators must maintain a record of what was shared, with whom, and when. In the America Prepared Campaign, a checklist is provided for principals and school leaders to identify areas that have been taken care of and those that need to be addressed. The list and other emergency preparedness guidelines can be accessed at http://www.workplaceviolence911.com/docs/20040916.pdf.

DOMAIN IV   **COLLABORATING WITH KEY STAKEHOLDERS**

COMPETENCY 010   **COLLABORATE WITH FAMILIES AND OTHER COMMUNITY MEMBERS**

Skill 10.1   **Accesses and utilizes resources of the school, family members, and community to affect student and adult learning, with a focus on removing barriers to learning**

A school does not rely solely on the school board and teachers for support. There are many outside agencies involved in the operation of a school. School leaders must learn how to harness the power of the surrounding community and its citizens. For instance, local law enforcement agents may visit a school to make safety presentations to students. They also like to make their presence known so students can seek help if they need it. This allows local officers to build relationships with students and the school community; which further benefits the community.

Health professionals also support the school. Nurses, speech pathologists, social workers, and mental health practitioners can help students as part of the school system or through external agencies. They come into the school on a regular basis or as they are needed to help both students and teachers. Local businesses, parents, and family members also have a role to play. Parents want to know what is happening in the school and they can be involved through the parent council. They are also visible in the school as volunteers helping teachers in the classroom or serving as chaperones for field trips and events.

Businesses can provide funding for events or school projects or can participate in career-education programs. Extra resources can be accessed through governmental, civic, and philanthropic organizations. Students also benefit when schools network to organize free or low-cost enrichment programs in athletics, fine arts, mentoring, or tutoring.

Not only are families strengthened when the school engages them and taps their human capital, they also reap long-term benefits when they attend community education programs for parents and family members. Regardless of their socio-economic status, families typically underestimate the importance of being involved in their children's education. For children who are performing well, the school can help parents identify ways to foster a love of learning. When children have difficulty, teachers and parents can work together to identify the learning barriers. They can then form a team to adopt and implement strategies to overcome the barriers.

<u>**10.1 A**</u>   **Collaborates with key stakeholders to utilize resources and assure barriers to learning are removed**

Initial contacts for resources outside of the school system will usually come from within the system itself, from administration, teacher organizations, department heads, and other colleagues. Resources can include libraries, museums, zoos, planetariums, etc. Teachers can obtain materials, media, speakers, and presenters from:

- Nonprofit organizations
- Social clubs
- Societies
- Civic organizations
- Community outreach programs of private businesses, corporations, and governmental agencies

Departments of social services can provide information relevant to social issues that may serve as barriers to individual student learning. In turn, this can be a resource for classroom instruction regarding life skills, at-risk behaviors, and related areas.

<u>**10.1 B**</u>   **Integrates a variety of programs and services, fully engaging the school and the entire community**

In the early days of American public education, teachers usually lived with one of the families in the community, and the community itself felt a strong sense of ownership in the school. The feeling of ownership has lost some of its vigor as public education has become more organized, has involved political entities at higher levels, and gets more funding from local sources.

Nevertheless, because schools are still owned by the people, using them as resources helps everyone. It brings the community into the school and increases a sense of ownership and community pride. In most effective schools, community members take a lot of interest in the schools and their welfare; they constantly work to bring the two closer together. Continuing education courses are popular examples of community/school initiatives. These classes invite the community into the building to develop interests or skills they might not be able to support otherwise.

Sports teams are another way the school engages the larger community. The school system can encourage the community to take pride and ownership in its teams. Sports award-events are typically well-attended and provide the opportunity for other extracurricular activities to be publicized. For instance the orchestra and choir could be employed to perform the national anthem. Likewise, student government can be enlisted to help plan the event and distribute the awards. In providing meeting space for blood drives and elections, the building becomes a community hub. School gyms may be the biggest meeting rooms in the city or county and can be utilized for large or small meetings.

Skill 10.2   Involves families in decision making about their children's education

Administrators must maintain a plethora of resources to deal with an ever-changing landscape of learners and classroom environments. The educator's primary professional concern will always be for the students and for the development of their potential. In a student-centered learning environment, the goal is to provide the best education, richest learning experiences, and numerous avenues to academic success for all students. Principals support teachers in developing learning plans that are individualized to a student's skill levels and needs. By using pre- and post-assessment data, a teacher more effectively develops and maximizes each student's potential. The school leader also supports instructional teams and constant communications with parents.

In working with parents, respectful reciprocal communication facilitates the best outcomes. This is especially true if the leader truly respects the opinions and ideas of others. He or she must recognize that teachers have a closer relationship with students and parents are usually well versed in what is going on with their child. Bringing them into the decision-making process may lead to solutions and success beyond what the administrator could accomplish alone. A triangular partnership must exist between administrators, parents, and teachers. When decisions are made regarding the management of the child in the classroom, the decisions should be shared.

Skill 10.3   Uses effective public information strategies to communicate with families and community members (e.g., email, night meetings, multiple languages)

See Skill 2.4

10.3 A   Understands and models the need for two-way communication

See Skill 2.4 A and Skill 2.4 B

Skill 10.4   Applies communication and collaboration strategies to develop positive family and local community partnerships, including recognizing and celebrating educational success

See Skill 3.3

10.4 A   Organizes internal and external venues and practices to celebrate the school and student success

See Skill 10.1 B

Skill 10.5   Utilizes appropriate strategies for communicating effectively with the media

Public relations must be carefully organized and it must be crafted for the public and the media. Information deliverers must have accurate information, understand their roles in disseminating information, and provide appropriate channels for feedback. The public must perceive that they are being given complete, timely information by officials who respect their feelings and sincerely want feedback. They must have an established frame of reference, i.e., know the schools' vision/mission statements, goals and objectives, and legislative issues that affect the local educational system.

Also see Skill 10.5 B

10.5 A   Uses a communication plan shared with key stakeholders

THE PUBLIC RELATIONS PROCESS

Public information management requires analyzing the community attitude toward educational issues. The required school improvement surveys conducted each spring in many schools provide not only feedback on the issues but priorities for addressing them. Public workshops and meetings allow community members to become involved in learning about budgetary, disciplinary, and academic issues. Information gathering should be structured to obtain the most scientific results. For instance, a representative sampling is more likely to be obtained from mailing surveys than from entrusting their delivery and return to students.

The planning phase requires setting specific goals and designing a campaign to achieve these goals. During this phase, educational leaders should determine the audiences, forums, and time frames in which their message(s) will be delivered to the public. For instance, presentations to senior citizens concerning a tax increase may require a different slant than a presentation to parents with children in the schools. Issues that require voter decisions should be presented with ample time for study and cooperative decision making, or at least discussion.

Following the communication process is equally important, whether information is delivered internally or externally. Student groups are a segment of the internal public and should be treated with the same open respect as other stakeholders. The information campaign must be encoded with specific audiences in mind. Especially important is selection of the media, or the transmission methods, for conveying the message. First-level media are usually in the form of newsletters to parents, press releases, and annual reports—any written document that can be distributed to the intended audiences. Follow-up transmissions include open houses, school committee or school board meetings, and educational fairs—any face-to-face communication that brings the public and school representatives together for a two-way exchange.

Finally, school/district officials must evaluate the results of the public relations effort. Some evaluation is immediate, as in the defeat of a candidate or the passage of a bond issue. Less timely feedback can be obtained through periodic evaluations such as brief questionnaires in school newsletters, telephone surveys, or written assessments at the end of public meetings to help test the public's understanding or the level of community support.

10.5 B Demonstrates an ability to communicate with the media

ESTABLISHING A GOOD RELATIONSHIP WITH THE MEDIA

Schools must establish good relationships with the media. When there are more educationally focused complaints in the Letters to the Editor section of the newspaper than there are news articles about school events, there is obviously poor interaction between the news media and the schools.

Of course, there are several other reasons for the amount of educational coverage provided by various media.

- Small, hometown newspapers give broader coverage to local issues/events. They may devote a whole page or section to school/classroom events.

- Newspapers have to evaluate the newsworthiness of various stories. Local spelling bees get better coverage than the mock trial in Ms. Clarke's debate class because one spelling bee winner in each district will compete nationally. Most newspapers consider a story of vandalism or fire at a school or a union walkout to be more newsworthy than a piece about students working at an animal shelter. Large city newspapers and television stations focus more on national and state news and regrettably often focus on educational issues that are negative or sensational.

- Local radio and television stations may be a better venue for school news; interviews with school officials, teachers, or students; or debates on education issues that have local impact.

School and/or district publications may be more useful in providing a positive link with the community, for example, newsletters, information brochures, handbooks, and annual reports. Also, displays of student work in public places provide visual evidence of student achievement, for example, in malls, building lobbies, and business waiting rooms.

COMPETENCY 011   COMMUNITY INTERESTS AND NEEDS

Skill 11.1   Identifies key stakeholders within the school community, including individuals and groups with competing perspectives

See Skill 2.1

Skill 11.2   Engages with the local community in a proactive manner

See Skill 10.1 B

11.2 A   Participates, actively and regularly, in a variety of community events as a school community representative

The school leader must engage community representatives to attend meetings and advise the school about neighborhood interests. Likewise, the leader must devote time and resources to the community. Block club meetings, local church events, and children's activities are all opportunities for the school to support neighborhood activism.

This reciprocal engagement also helps the school tackle its problems. Some issues are related to the larger community and require knowledge beyond the school building. For example, if drugs are allegedly being sold blocks from a school and students are supposedly making purchases during the lunch hour, information should be obtained. For this type of problem, community involvement is critical.

In a similar way, the educational leader must be able to network with individuals at the district level and with organizations that can provide important information. For instance, many school districts use the cohort-survival method to project student populations for future years. This formula, which considers current enrollment, local births, mobility rates, and new home construction, provides the school district with a population estimate that can be used for planning purposes. By maintaining an ongoing relationship and dialogue with local community organizations, religious institutions, realtors, and politicians, administrators can obtain valuable information concerning shifts in populations.

11.2 B   Advocates for the school within the community

An advocate is defined as a person who speaks or writes in support or defense of a person or cause. Principals have a responsibility to act as advocates for the schools and children they serve every day. To advocate effectively, educators must continually represent the school and make its interest a priority for parents and community members. This is another reason for principals and teachers to attend community events, particularly meetings of organizations who contribute to the school. When the school is represented, it is more likely to be supported rather than viewed as disconnected and unworthy of being funded.

Skill 11.3   Uses appropriate assessment strategies and research methods to understand and accommodate diverse student and community dynamics

As highlighted in Skill 4.1 C, educators must use performance data to identify diverse student needs. For most states or school districts there is an office of assessment and accountability that can provide data that are stratified by gender, race, or other variables. By reviewing these data on a regular basis, educational leaders can be aware of the dynamics of their students and can help to develop instructional strategies to overcome any challenges or barriers to learning. The educational leader must also be an active presence in the community. If he or she is actively engaged, then neighborhood leaders will remember to keep the school in-the-loop as they become aware of important issues both good and bad. The leader can then engage the appropriate team members to develop necessary plans and strategies.

<u>11.3 A</u>   **Accesses a variety of information sources to continuously learn more about the community and to develop an awareness of trends**

The school leader must devote a certain amount of time to reading the newspaper, particularly articles that deal with education. In addition, his or her eyes must be open to changes in the neighborhoods and ears must pick up on tidbits of information that deserve further investigation. If there are newsletters or email updates sent by block clubs or civic organizations, the principal should be on the list to receive these on a regular basis. Reading the information may be delegated to a secretary or even a student group who would be responsible for summarizing each item. With this written report, the principal can quickly note which items he or she needs to access and read in their entirety.

Skill 11.4   Utilizes diversity representative of the community to strengthen educational programs and planning

Schools are complex social systems involving a diverse range of students and teachers. Principals are successful when they can find ways to ensure that all students' sociological, linguistic, and cultural concerns are addressed.

SOCIOLOGICAL ISSUES

Sociological issues are highly important in schools. To understand children, educators must understand the society in which they live. Children will bring their own individual strengths and challenges. Even when they are the same age, no two children are alike. They will be at different stages of development and will have their own emotional and physical transformations that must be accommodated. These personal issues are compounded by sociological factors such as economic instability, neighborhood poverty, and violence both in the community and at school. It is clear that schools have many issues to deal with beyond student achievement.

Schools must be places where students feel safe, accepted, and valued. This is particularly true in the more challenging phases of student development, such as adolescence. At all ages, but particularly as students become more socially conscious, bullying is an issue. In recent years educators, researchers, and parents have brought bullying to the forefront of public discourse. As a result, numerous organizations, individuals, and governmental agencies have provided resources to address the issue. Among them is the federal government's website at http://www.stopbullying.gov/topics/get_help/index.html. It provides a list of resources including tips for identifying bullying and resources to get help.

To address bullying and other sociological issues, the principal must work with a team of stakeholders, especially parents and community groups. The team must establish, publish, and publicize a code of conduct so that everyone knows the campus must be safe, secure, and welcoming for all students. In addition, when violators are reprimanded and then punished in a swift and just way, all community members will understand that mean, discriminatory, dangerous, and illegal activities are not tolerated under any circumstances.

LINGUISTIC ISSUES

Linguistic issues are critical in a population that is increasingly diverse. Students come from various cultures and often speak different languages at home. While bilingual and English as a Second Language (ESL) learning programs deal directly with the academic issues of second-language learners, the school culture is also important.

Often, the message that students get at school is that in classrooms (where bilingual support is provided), second-language learners are valued. But, when they get out of the classroom and try to participate in the life of the school (activities, student government, athletics, etc.), they are not valued. This incongruity does a great disservice to these students as they then feel separate from the school culture. Principals must make sure that all second-language learners feel that they are part of the whole school at all times. Working with activities directors, support personnel, and faculty encourages this.

CULTURAL ISSUES

Cultural issues are important in multiple ways. First, teachers must be sensitive to students' cultural biases and assumptions in the classroom. Culturally relevant instruction is a concept that has become very important to public schooling in recent years. It suggests that because students come from different cultures, they will learn in different ways. Teachers, therefore, must be attentive to students' background knowledge, culture, religion, sexual orientation, etc. Even if some demographic information is not known about students, teachers need to be aware that all learners will see information in different ways. While each academic area has learning standards that must be met, there are many ways for students to learn and come to understand that information. Principals can model cultural-relevance with teachers. They should also continually encourage teachers and students to consider the perspectives of others.

11.4 A   **Involves members of diverse community groups in all school planning and improvement efforts**

See Skill 2.2 A, Skill 2.2 B, and Skill 11.4 A

Skill 11.5   **Demonstrates cultural sensitivity and competence by engaging communities in shared responsibilities that improve education and achievement of all students**

See Skill 11.4

COMPETENCY 012   MAXIMIZING COMMUNITY RESOURCES

Skill 12.1   Collaborates with community agencies that provide health, social, and other services to families and children

See Skill 10.1

Skill 12.2   Develops mutually beneficial relationships with business, religious, political, and service organizations to share both school and community resources such as buildings, playing fields, parks, and medical clinics

See Skill 2.1 B, Skill 10.1 A, and Skill 10.1 B

12.2 A   Identifies and documents the relationships and ensures equitable and open access to all groups in all venues as required or legally permissible

Schools operate in an Open System Model where external influences impact the effectiveness of the school-based administration and leadership. External influences provide input into the system of schooling in the form of people, policies, values, laws, technology, and other material resources. This input directly or indirectly affects not only school business decisions such as finance and purchasing, but also affects other functions of school operation such as the curriculum, pupil services, and the like.

School administrators must be aware of the various dimensions of educational politics in school districts; among these are politics of the community, politics of the state and the federal government, politics of the profession, politics of the local board of education, and politics of the bureaucracy (Kimbrough and Nunnery 1988). Perhaps the most important politics for school-based administrators are the politics of the community and its power structure, as well as identifying methods to analyze these structures and develop a plan to work with these groups. Additionally, practicing administrators must understand the politics involved in the process of educational policy development at the state and district levels.

The school organizational structure is greatly affected by existing conditions in the local community such as customs, traditions, and value systems. These conditions affect the power that is exercised on the formal and informal decision making process at the school district and school building levels. The biggest challenge is to identify the main power brokers in the community and learn how to work with them.

Administrators must be careful to balance their knowledge of the power brokers with their ethical responsibility to treat everyone equitable and fairly. It is important to reinforce the policy that everyone is respected, all needs are heard and considered, and everyone receives the same treatment. Having formal, documented processes will help ensure that this happens. When there is a system that has been developed by a team of stakeholders, then it is easier to enforce the steps necessary to make a determination. For instance, when groups request use of a meeting room, the secretary can provide the adopted request form and the appropriate school representative can make his or her decision "by the book". This ensures that equity and fairness prevail over preferences and special interests.

Skill 12.3 Uses resources from the community appropriately and effectively to support student learning

The principal is the gatekeeper of a school's resources. These include the non-monetary components such as human resources provided by staff, parents, and volunteers. Material resources are also valuable and necessary to support school functioning and student learning.

12.3 A Evaluates the effective use of current community resources in support of student learning

To ensure proper resource allocation and accounting, districts and/or states define the purchase value that requires the administrators or principals signature. Whenever a purchase exceeds the specified amount, the administrator must approve and sign for it to be procured. Another wise strategy requires that spending be guided by the campus improvement plan and that a committee of stakeholders oversee expenditures. The team should be comprised of members representing the school staff, parents, and other members of the school community. For example, if funds are requested for an autism conference, but there are no school goals or student needs in this area, then this request should not be funded. However, if the school goals include literacy development, then a request for funding for additional library books may be approved.

The principal also controls the human resources, or staffing the school. School staffing models vary from district to district, but all principals have some control over how many teachers and support staff members are hired. Principals may make decisions about job descriptions, duties, assigned responsibilities, appraisals, and professional development.

An important waste-avoidance process occurs in the human resource category. Rather than having ineffective staff members continue on the payroll, principals must document and remove employees who do not contribute to the school goals. When additional support is needed, before hiring new individuals, the principal must assess how current staff is being used. He or she may find that the need can be filled by reallocating team members. For example, when teachers are absent and there are not enough substitute teachers to cover the classes, the principal must decide how to manage the classes by combining students or by reassigning office staff or support staff to fill this need.

Resources are always limited, and conflict can occur when stakeholders are denied their requests for spending. Involving the school leadership team in these decisions and keeping the group focused on student achievement will help the principal maintain integrity and will keep the focus on the school vision.

Skill 12.4   Seeks community support to sustain existing resources and identifies additional resources as needed

See Skill 8.5 and Skill 10.1

<u>12.4 A</u>   Provides information to the community about the benefit of existing and needed resources

See Skill 2.4

<u>12.4 B</u>   Identifies and solicits community resources to support student learning

See Skill 10.1, Skill 10.1 A, and Skill 10.1 B

DOMAIN V   **ETHICS AND INTEGRITY**

COMPETENCY 013   **ETHICAL AND LEGAL BEHAVIOR**

Skill 13.1 **Models personal and professional ethics, integrity, justice, and fairness, and expects the same of others**

Principals are leaders. Their behavior and stated and implied communications have a tremendous impact on those with whom they work. Others often follow the lead of the principal. If a principal behaves with strong professional ethics and integrity, the faculty, staff, students, and parents will usually assume this position; the reverse is also true.

Management of a school requires a clear understanding of the importance of public perception, as well as techniques to handle successes and challenges. It is often effective to establishing a public relations committee. In consultation with the principal, this group shares positive and negative messages in an honest and direct manner. Brochures, speaking engagements, and student presentations are successful and low cost ways to share good news. Cultivating a friendly relationship with all local media benefits a school. This opens the door for good news to be reported and for the principal to be interviewed when bad news must be tempered. The public relations committee can also prepare press releases to share the "good news" about the school.

It has been said that perception is reality. The importance of perceptions by a school's community can never be overlooked. If the school is to be perceived in a positive light, it must control negative information about the students, staff, faculty, administration, and other elements. The best control strategy is to remove situations that create negativism. Additionally, the physical appearance of the school's building and grounds, as well as the behavior and achievements of its students, contribute to the school's image.

School principals are faced with numerous ethical issues at both the classroom and building level. Keeping this in mind, principals must continuously reflect upon the decisions they make and the examples they set for their students, parents, and colleagues. An effective school principal will investigate different strategies to address ethical dilemmas. He/she will then work to develop the skills and dispositions needed to handle ethical challenges. Current ethical issues include:

- High-stakes testing
- Special education
- Zero-tolerance policies
- Teacher evaluation/merit pay.
- Separation of church and state
- Creationism vs. evolution
- Teaching contracts and teacher tenure
- The right to due process

School leaders must deal with ethical issues in a professional manner. Additionally, he/she must follow all applicable laws and policies and be aware of legal precedents.

13.1 A   Behaves in a trustworthy manner

A leader who resolves conflict in a systematic, fair manner promotes this kind of behavior within the school. In addition, others closely observe and follow the way a principal shares information and reaches decisions. The administrator who shows partiality or insists that his or her position is the only one will not obtain meaningful input from those with whom he or she is working. In this type of environment, people will behave in ways that are not collegial. They either affirm the principal's views, say what they think the principal wants to hear, or they say nothing and become disillusioned or detached. This produces poor results because collaborative processes are not a part of the planning, implementation, or evaluation.

A strong principal realizes that there are times when executive decisions must be made and he/she makes them in a timely fashion. For example, if a person enters the campus with a gun, the principal must take action to safeguard everyone. Likewise, if teachers are in conflict, the school leader must resolve the problem quickly before it deters from achieving the organizational goals. When the principal is guided by the collegially-adopted campus vision and goals, then it is easier to obtain support for executive decisions that may otherwise be challenged. Even if there are persistent challenges, the leader can typically close the matter by clearly communicating the link between the decisions and the school goals.

It is not pleasant when rules and consequences must be enforced. However, backlash is lessened when there is a code of conduct or ethics that have been adopted by a team of stakeholders. When the code has been breached, then its rules specify what consequences should be enacted. At times the principal may feel that the prescribed punishment exceeds the crime. In no case should the code be "bent" for an individual or a particular situation. Rather, the committee should be reconvened and the leader should present the evidence for why the code should be altered. This shows respect and maintains the integrity of the collegial decision-making process. At all times, the school community must see the principal behaving ethically, justly, and professionally. Only then will the leader maintain the respect, trust, and support of his or her stakeholders.

13.1 B   Recognizes when ethics have been breached and takes appropriate action

Principals must exercise caution and always consider ethical and legal implications when dealing with all constituents, especially students, faculty, staff, parents, and the media. The threat of a lawsuit is always present. However, when administrators treat people fairly, implement policies and procedures consistently, and keep proper documentation, they do not need to be anxious. Additionally, effective principals will try to anticipate problems and prevent situations from escalating.

When issues arise, teachers, students, and parents will be looking to the principal. He or she must ensure that situations are handled professionally and within the laws and guidelines. If the school leader maintains a collaborative environment that is open, honest, and consistent, the vast majority of issues can be resolved through dialogue and compromise.

Principals should be well aware of the laws, policies, and procedures that are most likely to affect them. Many districts provide this information on their websites and through professional development sessions. On a regular basis, administrators must also review legal and procedural updates at the federal, state, or district level. Pertinent information must then be disseminated to the faculty, staff, students, parents, and other parties who need to remain informed.

THE CODE OF CONDUCT

As highlighted in Skill 11.4, a code of conduct is an important document. First, it should be developed by a team of stakeholders. Since the final product is collaboratively designed, it has the legitimacy of being agreed upon by representatives from all groups within the school community. Second, the code provides a litmus test by which behaviors can be measured and addressed. Lastly, the code of conduct must include pre-determined steps for dealing with violators. If a situation arises and the code cannot provide adequate guidance, then the committee must be reconvened to update the code. When the code is enforced consistently and swiftly, then the school community is reminded that everyone is expected to behave in ways that are ethical and acceptable.

<u>13.1 C</u>   Holds self and others accountable for ethical behavior

See Skill 13.1 A

Skill 13.2   Ensures and monitors the use of appropriate systems and procedures to protect the rights and confidentiality of all students and staff

Many states include confidentiality in their educational code of ethics. This means that administrators cannot share confidential information unless it serves a lawful professional purpose or is required by law. Maintaining confidentiality is of the utmost importance in the school setting. If students, parents, or staff members know that important information can be kept confidential, this can promote more active participation in the school community. One existing federal law that deals with confidentiality in schools is FERPA, the Family Educational Rights and Privacy Act. This legislation governs the disclosure of students' educational records.

In addition to traditional issues of confidentiality, administrators face new issues as part of the information age. Important decisions include who should and should not have access to certain records. Security is always an issue when significant amounts of information are stored in one location. This is the case with computerized databases and electronic files of sensitive information. Parameters must be clearly developed and monitored so that authorized users cannot disseminate information in ways that violate confidentiality and breach professional ethics. Network security is a serious and time-intensive task that the school leader should delegate to someone who is professionally trained. This individual, and if necessary, his/her team, should report to the administrator and be responsible for monitoring the network and addressing threats such as hackers, viruses, and outages.

Skill 13.3   Uses the influence of the position to enhance education and the common good (e.g., social justice)

Research has long supported the idea that high-quality education provides societal benefits. In highlighting the government's investment in education, U.S. Secretary of Education Arne Duncan said "If we want to strengthen the American workforce, we must continue to invest in education."[2] For a nation to thrive it must have high levels of secondary schooling; education fuels economic growth and fosters societal development. In the United States, educational attainment is one of the top measures of social class.

For all these reasons, educational leaders must not only work to educate current students, they must also advance the cause of education to the public. School leaders must highlight that a free democratic society depends on responsible, thoughtful, and innovative citizens. The administration has to support teachers who embrace the challenges and rewards of educating all children. This cannot be done from behind a desk or even by having in-house celebrations for the school's great achievements. An educational leader must also be an ambassador by attending community events, participating in meetings, and joining important organizations.

To share their message with varied audiences, school leaders must respect diversity, know ethical principles, understand political theories, and speak about economic issues. It also requires that educators have an understanding of who children are — both as individuals and as members of society. Often students serve as the most pervasive ambassadors for their schools and for education as a whole. Therefore, principals and teachers must ensure that the school is a haven where all children can learn and grow to love learning. The curriculum should teach each child about becoming a responsible citizen and the adults in the school must model and reinforce this type of behavior daily.

Skill 13.4   Reinforces transparent (open) decision-making practices by making data and rationales explicit

See Skill 2.4

---

[2] Accessed 2/21/2012 from http://www.ed.gov/news/press-releases/us-department-education-2013-budget-continues-investments-strengthen-workforce-a

13.4 A   **Communicates reasons for decisions as appropriate**

See Skill 2.4 and Skill 2.4 A

13.4 B   **Develops a plan to facilitate an open decision making process**

See Skill 2.5

13.4 C   **Disseminates data in a transparent or open manner within legal constraints**

See Skill 1.1 A

COMPETENCY 014   PERSONAL VALUES AND BELIEFS

Skill 14.1   Demonstrates respect for the inherent dignity and worth of each individual

An effective, collegial school must value and respect each of its members whether they are faculty, staff, parents, students, or community members. Everyone needs and deserves to be treated with respect, whether they are from the mayor's office or are a part of the custodial staff. In particular, staff members need to know that the administration is there to help in any situation, will respect confidential information, and does not show favoritism.

Several strategies should be developed by administrators who want to foster this type of environment. They include:

- Utilizing strong communication skills
- Fostering collegiality, civility, and respect
- Creating a system of rewards and recognition
- Developing effective teams
- Establishing trust
- Managing stressful situations
- Supporting staff in times of change

When a new administrator comes into a school, he or she has to develop a sense of trust with the staff. They need to know that the administrator will support them when they face problems with students, parents, or other co-workers. Staff members who do an exceptional job need to be recognized and this should be done publicly, for example, at staff meetings. The administrator should look for exemplary teaching or behavior in all staff, but at the same time rewards and recognition should not be handed out frivolously.

Also see Skill 2.2 B

Skill 14.2   Models respect for diversity and treating others equitably

See Skill 12.2 A

Skill 14.3   Establishes and maintains an open and inclusive school community

See Skill 4.3 and Skill 4.3 B

Skill 14.4   Uses a variety of strategies to lead others in safely examining deeply held assumptions and beliefs that may conflict with the school's vision and goals

See Skill 2.2

14.4 A   **Assesses the school culture to determine if there are negative deeply held assumptions and beliefs that could impact teaching and learning**

Every human system has its own culture, traditions, and norms. These long-held components are often based on assumptions and beliefs that can be harnessed to achieve newly adopted visions and goals. In some cases, however, system-wide assumptions may be detrimental to the current direction of the organization. In an educational institution assumptions will exist regarding innumerable factors including the nature of education, who should teach and who should learn, and which children are most worthy of receiving the investment of educational resources.

This last area is especially difficult to uncover for several reasons. The primary one is that most stakeholders have superficially adopted the idea that all children can and should learn; however, few have sufficiently been prepared for the task of making this concept a reality. In order for the educational environment to effectively support all learners, individuals must be open and honest about their beliefs and assumptions. Only truthful data can reveal the assumptions that need to be addressed and replaced. To collect honest and accurate information, a valid and reliable instrument should be anonymously collected from administrators, faculty, staff, parents, and if applicable, students. Once the results have been analyzed and reviewed, then the school can engage in what Peter Senge calls the 'Dance of Change'.

A more informal process can involve activities during staff workshops or PTSA meetings. During these sessions the team can engage in brainstorming tasks such as listing five adjectives to describe the school. Everyone would then work to organize the adjectives into themes and then identify which themes are positive and which are negative. In future sessions brainstorming work can help identify factors that helped foster the positive areas. The team can also discuss the negative areas, factors that encourage the problems, and how to overcome the challenges.

This strategy will be superficial if the team members do not feel supported and respected. Even in a collegial environment, it may be necessary to set and commit to ground rules that encourage authenticity and honesty. In their 2009 article in the Journal of Leadership Education, Timothy Galpin and J. Lee Whittington suggest simple ground rules such as:

- Stay on topic
- Do not over participate
- Agree to disagree
- Listen
- Respect others' ideas
- Be brief

The Society for Organizational Learning (SoL) suggests the following three steps:

- Becoming more aware of your own thinking and reasoning (reflection);
- Making your thinking and reasoning more visible to others (advocacy);
- Inquiring into others' thinking and reasoning (inquiry).

The SoL also suggests that everyone has Mental Models, or beliefs, attitudes, perceptions, and assumptions. Mental modes, or assumptions, can often be effective in helping people respond to other people and things that they encounter, particularly things that are new. However, assumptions can prevent people from achieving their goals because assumptions are based on four factors that are not always accurate, they are:

- Our beliefs are the truth.
- The truth is obvious.
- Our beliefs are based on real data.
- The data we select are the real data.

The leader can encourage his or her team to engage in constant reflection about their mental modes. Each person should also make a concerted effort to avoid judging the words or actions of others. Instead, open communication should be encouraged. For both parties to come to the same conclusions, listeners must ask questions to see if the sender's message (the person's statement or action), was what was concluded (the listener's interpretation of the statement or action). In some cases, the conclusion may be in error and it can then be corrected. At other times the sender may have erroneous assumptions or beliefs. Through reflection and inquiry, the sender may recognize his or her inaccurate assumptions, and can be supported in changing them.

Skill 14.5   Challenges assumptions and beliefs respectfully as they may adversely affect students and adults

See Skill 14.4 A

14.5 A   Recognizes factors that may adversely affect students and adults and takes appropriate action

See Skill 14.4 A

14.5 B   Assesses the school culture to determine if there are negative deeply held assumptions and beliefs that could impact students and adults

See Skill 14.4 A, Skill 3.3, and Skill 3.6 A

COMPETENCY 015 HIGH STANDARDS FOR SELF AND OTHERS

Skill 15.1 Reflects upon own work, analyzes strengths and weaknesses, and establishes goals for professional growth

See Skill 4.7

<u>15.1 A</u> **Develops a personal plan for professional growth and development**

A school leader must establish personal and professional goals for the same reason that goals are developed for the school and its teachers and students. After creating goals, a professional-development plan is created. This document links goals with strengths and weaknesses that need to be addressed. The superintendent or principal can often overlook his or her own professional growth because there are so many other areas where attention must be paid.

To avoid this pitfall, the principal should create a plan with milestones and deliverables that coincide with those set for his or her teachers. For instance, if teachers must report on their professional-development plan each month, the principal should also do the same. Many districts support leadership development by placing administrators in cohorts. Leaders are then able to support, encourage, and push one another.

This strategy is even more structured for schools that have been identified as under-performing. When a school fails to meet benchmarks established by the federal-government, state, or district, the School Improvement Plan (SIP) must include procedures for increasing the principal's ability to lead the school in its turn-around efforts. This is the extreme case of mandated professional growth; effective leaders are not driven by consequences but by a desire to be the best that they can be. To do this, professional growth and development must always receive appropriate attention, time, and resources.

Skill 15.2 Models and encourages continuous professional growth

See Skill 4.2, Skill 4.3, Skill 4.5, and Skill 4.5 B

Skill 15.3 Administers educational policies equitably and legally

See Skill 13.1 B

Skill 15.4 Refocuses attention on vision and goals when controversial issues arise

Inevitably, problems occur and controversies arise. The quality of the problem-solving strategy determines the longevity of the proposed solution and the probable recurrence of the same or similar difficulties. At all times, even during times of crises, an educational leader must keep the school's pre-determined plans at the forefront of everyone's minds. This is particularly the case when the team is focused on solving problems that seem unrelated to the vision and goals. These core planning tools can serve as roadmaps and can ensure that distractions do not divert the school from its charted course.

Also see Skill 4.4 A

15.4 A Develops a process that involves all stakeholders on refocusing attention on vision and goals

See Skill 2.3 and Skill 2.5

15.4 B Holds others accountable for ethical behavior

See Skill 13.1 A

DOMAIN VI   THE EDUCATIONAL SYSTEM

COMPETENCY 016   PROFESSIONAL INFLUENCES

Skill 16.1   Facilitates constructive discussions with the school community about local, state, and federal laws, policies, regulations, and statutory requirements

See Skill 1.3 and Skill 1.4 B

16.1 A   Explains policies and regulations to the school community

Schools should welcome the opportunity to educate not only students, but all members of the community. There will be issues that must be explained to parents, community groups, and business leaders. It is a wise school leader who capitalizes on the chance to engage stakeholders by teaching them about educational policies, regulations, and trends.

For most stakeholders, federal, state, or district policies only receive attention when there are urgent or unpleasant regulations to be enacted. Principals can mitigate this trend by posting regular updates of school board meetings or actions. A bulletin board can also be devoted to sharing educational news, links, and resources.

16.1 B   Listens to questions and problems and interacts with the school community to increase understanding

If a particularly controversial issue needs to be presented, a town-hall meeting can be held so that the policies can be discussed and explained. Two-way communication should be facilitated; the agenda should allocate time for attendees to voice their concerns and evaluations can be used to collect feedback. As the meeting transitions to an end, the agenda should highlight events or strategies that the school is using to achieve its vision and goals.

To make the best use of time and resources, information should be shared electronically via email, websites, and blogs. This gives ongoing, instant access to users, and provides a location for directing inquiries. Persistent issues or repetitive questions should be documented so that a Frequently Asked Questions (FAQ) document can be created and shared. Despite all these strategies, some members of the school community will still want to have face-to-face interface with the school leader. The principal must always be ready to listen, respond, and provide the type of interaction that meets the needs of his or her constituents.

Skill 16.2 **Develops relationships with stakeholders and policymakers to identify, respond to, and influence issues, trends, and potential changes that affect the context and conduct of education**

See Skill 13.3, Skill 11.2 A, and Skill 11.2 B

Skill 16.3 **Advocates for equity and adequacy in providing for students and families' needs (educational, physical, emotional, social, cultural, legal, and economic) to meet educational expectations and policy requirements**

See Skill 8.3, Skill 11.4, Skill 10.1, and 10.1 A

COMPETENCY 017 **MANAGING LOCAL DECISIONS WITHIN THE LARGER EDUCATIONAL POLICY ENVIRONMENT**

Skill 17.1 Communicates data about educational performance to inform decision-making and improve policy

Data are most useful when shared in a timely and understandable manner. In education, the most important data are those that highlight how students are performing in various domains. Although accountability requirements focus heavily on the cognitive domain, the school should also find ways to share information about other areas such as students' social and emotional development. When sharing information about cognitive development, the school should prepare messages that are geared to specific audiences. For instance, when communicating how a child performed on the quarterly standardized assessment, a different set of information should be shared with parents than what is shared with teachers.

After the information is shared, specific actions can be taken to engage the appropriate decision- and policy-makers. One strategy could be holding a series of meetings to solicit feedback and gather suggestions for celebrating successes and addressing challenges. Another strategy is to engage the curriculum design team so that they can process the data and propose a plan to address the identified gaps. To serve as an educational advocate, a school leader must also take the data and create a clear, yet concise, document that suggests ways in which policy decisions can support improvement efforts. This strategy is most effective when the leader has a well-known presence in the policy-making arena. Therefore, when a principal is active at the district, regional, state, and even federal level, it serves the long-term good of the school.

Also see Skill 1.1 A and Skill 2.4

17.1 A Engages in appropriate lobbying and political activism to communicate data about educational performance in order to inform decision-making and improve policy

As highlighted in skill 17.1 above, the school leader must have a presence in the policy-making arena. This may mean serving in a leadership capacity for appropriate civic or professional organizations. At the national level, there are numerous organizations including:

- The American Association of School Administrators - www.aasa.org
- American Association of School Personnel Administrators - http://www.aaspa.org
- American Educational Research Association - http://www.aera.net
- Association for Supervision and Curriculum Development - http://www.ascd.org
- A more complete list is provided by the U.S. Department of Education at http://www2.ed.gov/about/contacts/gen/othersites/associations.html.

These organizations provide excellent opportunities for educational leaders to engage in structured lobbying efforts, publish and present best practices, and network with other professionals. At the local or state level, policy-makers often seek the advice of principals and superintendents. By serving on roundtables and advisory groups, the school leader will be able to make data-driven and student-focused suggestions to improve decision-making and policy-setting processes.

Also see Skill 2.4 A

Skill 17.2 Communicates effectively with key decision makers to improve public understanding of local, state, and federal laws, policies, regulations, and statutory requirements

Educational leaders, specifically principals, have a valuable role as the intermediaries between policy makers and citizens. It is the principal who usually hears both the praises and the criticisms that parents have about a particular policy or regulation. Likewise, these leaders understand the day-to-day impact of educationally-focused legislation. This includes the ways in which laws affect students, teachers, families, communities, and the nation as a whole. For all of these reasons, administrators must be able to communicate with decision makers and with the public.

The administrator must first take the time to fully understand what is occurring at the federal, state, and local level. The more complex the rules, the more advisable it will be to attend workshops or conferences that will be taught by experts in the law. This is another benefit of being a member of professional organizations. Conferences will usually focus on new legislation, recent trends, and best practices that comply with requirements. State agencies and school districts also provide trainings to help busy administrators stay current and well-informed about important policies and practices.

For most administrators, it is a challenge to allocate time for meetings or trainings 'out-of-the-building'. However, attending these events is a more effective use of time compared to simply reading and re-reading complex legislative documents. The benefits can then be shared with teachers, staff members, parents, and community members. These stakeholders can learn about the laws and policies through administrator-planned meetings, newsletters, bulletin boards, and emails.

Also see Skill 16.1 A and 16.2

Skill 17.3 Advocates for excellence and equity in education

In this PRAXIS guide, previous skills highlighted reasons why administrators must serve as educational advocates. In addition, advocacy strategies have been highlighted throughout. When thinking specifically about excellence and equity, the administrator must advocate to two groups. The first group includes those who set policies and must be constantly reminded that all children must have access to high quality and rigorous education. This group includes legislators, court officials, and policy-makers. The second group includes those individuals who are impacted by requirements set by the first group. Students, teachers, parents, and community members fall into the second group.

When advocating to the first group, the educational leader should present data showing why society benefits when all children have access to high quality education. This argument is challenging, particularly during economically challenging times. During these seasons, fiscal decisions lean towards reducing rather than increasing funding for education. Therefore, administrators must make a strong case for why the wisest fiscal policy involves investing in a strong educational foundation.

Also see Skill 11.2 B and Skill 5.1

SAMPLE TEST

DOMAIN I VISION AND GOALS

1. An example of reliability in testing is:
   (Average) (Skill 1.1 B)

   A. Items on the test produce the same response each time
   B. The test was administered with poor lighting
   C. Items on the test measure what they should measure
   D. The test is too long for the time allotted

2. _____ is a standardized test in which performance is directly related to the educational objective(s)
   (Average) (Skill 1.1 B)

   A. An aptitude test
   B. A norm-referenced test
   C. A criterion-referenced test
   D. A summative evaluation

3. Fill in the blanks for I. ____ and II. ____ in the picture below:
   (Rigorous) (Skill 1.1 B)

   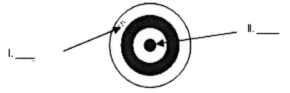

   A. I. Reliability and II. Validity
   B. I. Validity and II. Reliability
   C. I. Reliability and II. Vigor
   D. I. Rigor and II. Validity

4. Your district is considering implementing block scheduling in each of its high schools. As principal of one of these schools and a strong advocate of block scheduling, your best approach to involving the faculty in the decision-making process is to:
   (Easy) (Skill 1.2)

   A. Present only the advantages of block scheduling
   B. Present and invalidate all objections to block scheduling
   C. Present advantages and objections, relating each to the school's vision
   D. Present the school board position as inevitable and seek the best methods of implementing block scheduling at your school site

5. When implementing the selected vision and goals, the school leader must make sure they are aligned with:
   (Average) (Skill 1.2 A)

   A. Federal research
   B. Community town-hall meetings
   C. Student proposals
   D. State and district standards or requirements

6. Goals are often drafted using the SMART method. Which one of the following is NOT a component of this acronym?
   (Average) (Skill 1.2 C)

   A. Scorable
   B. Relevant
   C. Achievable
   D. Time-framed

7. At a community roundtable convened by the principal, business leaders expressed concern that they have been unable to hire recent graduates. They cite a lack of technological knowledge as the main reason why jobs could not be offered to the school's former students. The administration was able to identify this gap because they:
   (Easy) (Skill 2.1)

   A. Researched the Census Bureau's employment data
   B. Continued to engage students on Facebook™
   C. Engaged parents and other stakeholders from the community
   D. Administered surveys about the jobs held by parents

8. The district has adopted a new grading scale that is stricter than the state requirement. Which of the following would be the most <u>time-efficient</u> means of obtaining feedback from the community?
   (Easy) (Skill 2.4)

   A. Distributing an end-of-year school improvement survey
   B. Holding meetings with small groups of parent volunteers
   C. Delivering a presentation at a school board meeting
   D. Participating in an interview on a popular local radio station with responses to questions called in by listeners

9. Communication in which a school principal receives feedback from the faculty/staff is:
   (Easy) (Skill 2.4 A)

   A. Downward
   B. Lateral
   C. Upward
   D. Diagonal

10. Which of the following represents the proper sequential order in the communication process?
(Easy) (Skill 2.4 A)

    A. Ideating, decoding, transmitting, receiving, encoding, acting
    B. Ideating, encoding, transmitting, receiving, decoding, acting
    C. Ideating, transmitting, encoding, receiving, decoding, acting
    D. Ideating, encoding, transmitting, receiving, acting, decoding

11. The administration drafts the master plan of teaching assignments for the coming school year. This step will most likely increase teacher commitment to the vision and goal:
(Easy) (Skill 2.5)

    A. If the plan is finalized in time to notify teachers of their assignments before the end of the current school year
    B. If some teachers are members of the planning committee and if all teachers are able to provide input toward the final plan
    C. Even if last-minute changes have to be made before school opens
    D. Because they know that the administration is acting in good faith

12. In defining the _____ model, key values include respect and inclusion, collaboration, authenticity, and self-awareness
(Average) (Skill 2.5)

    A. organizational development
    B. theory of change
    C. practitioner's guide
    D. leadership initiative

13. Conducting _____ is the process of gathering information to identify and define the problem before initiating a project or program.
(Rigorous) (Skill 3.1)

    A. a survey
    B. a needs assessment
    C. an evaluation
    D. None of the above

14. When the administration is working to achieve the vision and goals of the school, which of the following strategies should they use?
(Average) (Skill 3.2)

    A. Analyze data specific to their school
    B. Read current educational research
    C. Visit a school that exemplifies the high test scores and vision of NCLB
    D. All of the above

15. Which of the following is a more LONG-TERM reason for teachers to facilitate productive, eager learners?
(Rigorous) (Skill 3.2)

A. These students cause fewer disruptions than students who are bored

B. These students apply new knowledge in class and in their life experiences

C. These students usually come from wealthier, more affluent families

D. All of the above

16. Some critics suggest that the original form of No Child Left Behind (NCLB) relied on external rather than internal motivation. What argument is used to support this position?
(Rigorous) (Skill 3.3)

A. It relied on the principle that rewards and punishments would increase motivational levels of teachers, principals, and students

B. It utilized incremental growth targets that were more intrinsic than extrinsic

C. The 2010 refinement of NCLB provides rewards for outstanding teachers and leaders

D. It sought to harness the external mechanisms that cause individuals to achieve, grow and develop, and reach their potential

17. At times, administrators must force teachers to change. What should a school principal do to help teachers adapt to forced change?
(Rigorous) (Skill 3.4)

A. Require teachers to adapt to changes quickly and with minimal negativity

B. Present all the changes together; this helps to engage in all change-acceptance processes at the same time

C. Gather data to help teachers make sense of why changes are necessary

D. Adhere to the dictates of a collegial environment; this may mean rejecting the change if the teachers are not in favor of it

18. Informal lateral communication does all of the following EXCEPT:
(Average) (Skill 3.6 A)

A. Serves as a vehicle for peer-to-peer communication

B. Provides a hierarchy through which information is distributed

C. Becomes a means of cohesion for team members

D. Facilitates sharing information quickly

DOMAIN II TEACHING AND LEARNING

19. **When preparing for individualized classroom instruction, which of the following strategies should be used?**
(Rigorous) (Skill 4.1 C)

    A. Give the same level of instruction to all students so that the same content is presented to everyone

    B. Exempt certain children whose special-needs conditions would reduce their ability to understand the content

    C. Provide a lengthier test period for the entire class to complete standardized assessments (i.e., provide everyone with four hours instead of three or two)

    D. None of the above

20. **Which of the following is MOST LIKELY to assist participants in staff development activities to retain information?**
(Easy) (Skill 4.2)

    A. Cover the topic in a single-session workshop

    B. Cover the topic in a three-to-four-session workshop

    C. Cover the topic throughout the school year, allowing teachers to try the strategies, and then report back

    D. Cover the topic daily at informal meetings

21. **Which of the following is the LEAST effective model of professional development?**
(Average) (Skill 4.2)

    A. Workshops held once per month which focus on the same topic for three months at a time

    B. An intensive one-day workshop with specific activities for teachers to implement in their classrooms

    C. Ongoing planning meetings to adapt new materials to the school

    D. Classroom assistance by resource personnel to assist with program implementation over time

22. **Between the two methods of motivation:**
(Average) (Skill 4.2 A)

    A. Extrinsic motivation is better; it is easy to find rewards to get teachers to perform

    B. Intrinsic motivation is better; teachers want to engage in professional development without needing rewards or punishments

    C. Extrinsic motivation is better; teachers are internally motivated

    D. Intrinsic motivation is better; teachers try to avoid punishments

23. To encourage a school environment that embraces change, the educational leader should do all of the following EXCEPT:
(Average) (Skill 4.3)

   A.   Model openness to change
   B.   Commit to using democratic processes to make all decisions
   C.   Collaborate with stakeholders to discuss the need for change
   D.   Demonstrate a willingness to change own position on an issue

24. Select the statement that best describes the table below.
(Rigorous) (Skill 4.4 A)

	High Relationship	Low Relationship
High Task Behavior	Organizational Mode	Crisis Mode
Low Task Behavior	Interpersonal Mode	Routine Mode

   A.   This table shows the four modes or strategies for developing individual goals
   B.   This table describes the four group problem-solving modes in situational leadership
   C.   This table is a replication of Fiedler's four-stage contingency theory
   D.   This table depicts the major steps in developing an MBO program

25. To encourage team-teaching, the administration should do which of the following:
(Average) (Skill 4.4 B)

   A.   Pair teachers by subject area rather than by grade level
   B.   Pair teachers by grade level rather than by subject area
   C.   Schedule the day so teachers have their prep periods at the same time
   D.   Schedule teachers to work in teams for a week-at-a-time

26. In _____ there is the belief that "the more power we share, the more power we have to use".
(Easy) (Skill 4.5)

   A.   collaborative leadership
   B.   democratic leadership
   C.   creative leadership
   D.   All of the above

27. Which of the following is a strategy to individualize instruction and make the student responsible for his or her own learning?
(Easy) (Skill 4.6 A)

   A.   A lesson plan
   B.   A learning contract
   C.   An administrative directive
   D.   A student study plan

28. **Administrators who engage in scholastic writing to share effective educational strategies are coveted in school districts. Why?**
(Rigorous) (Skill 4.7)

   A. It is important that administrators be able to communicate with others about effective strategies
   B. Administrators need time to reflect on their practice and scholastic writing is one way to present new paradigms and theoretical constructs
   C. To share effective educational strategies, the administrator must be aware, and likely utilize, best practices
   D. All of the above

29. **After three years of implementing its School Improvement Plan, School Five has learned that over 90% of its students mastered the mandated state standards and have performed at the proficient level on the state-required assessment. This is likely a result of:**
(Easy) (Skill 5.1)

   A. Shadowing a school in a neighboring state
   B. Focusing on research regarding future trends in math and reading
   C. Engaging parents to provide extracurricular enrichment activities
   D. Creating a school-wide commitment to standards-based instruction

30. **A school-based instructional team is developing learning objectives. Which of the following lists the top two areas they should consider?**
(Average) (Skill 5.1)

   A. Textbooks and bibliographies
   B. State-standards and students
   C. Teachers and administrators
   D. Parents and community groups

31. **Which of the following best illustrates an observable objective?**
(Average) (Skill 5.1)

   A. Eighty percent of students will be able to solve multiplication word problems at the rate of one problem per minute with 75 percent accuracy
   B. Students will appreciate the originality of cultural music
   C. Ten percent of the students will comprehend the implications of good health and physical fitness
   D. All of the above

32. **The best way to improve a school is to:**
(Easy) (Skill 5.1 C)

  A. Obtain a nationally recognized authority on the topic
  B. Involve teachers in initiating, planning, implementing, and evaluating the program
  C. Have teachers advertise the program
  D. Have the principal plan and let a few teachers review the plan

33. **_____ reviews the program environment and its met and unmet needs.**
(Average) (Skill 5.3)

  A. Content evaluation
  B. Input evaluation
  C. Process evaluation
  D. Product evaluation

34. **Which of the following refers to the horizontal organization of the elements of the curriculum?**
(Rigorous) (Skill 5.4 A)

  A. The knowledge and skills students learn are useful in life situations
  B. The knowledge and skills that students learn at one grade level are relevant and useful as they progress to other grades
  C. Everything the student learns contributes to fulfillment
  D. During a school year, what students learn in one class supports and reinforces what they learn in other classes during that same year

35. **The annual Campus Improvement Plan (CIP) or School Improvement Plan (SIP) should have all of the following EXCEPT:**
(Easy) (Skill 5.5 A)

  A. The school's goals
  B. Activities to accomplish the school's goals
  C. The personnel who monitored the previous school goals
  D. A timeline for completion of the goals

36. **Teachers may resist integrating technology for all of the following reasons EXCEPT:**
(Easy) (Skill 5.6)

A. Habit of doing the same things for years
B. Training and staff development
C. Preserving the status quo
D. Belief that the new idea will meld with their current beliefs or practices

37. **Mr. Blanchard has taken care to match the qualifications of new teachers he hires with school needs and district policies. However, by the end of the first semester, he has received numerous complaints about his new hires. Additionally some community leaders have criticized him for the school-wide changes he has implemented. From the information provided, what is a likely explanation for this criticism?**
(Rigorous) (Skill 5.7 B)

A. The new teachers did not buy into the school mission and vision
B. Students dislike the school vision and have complained to their parents about how the new teachers promote it
C. Mr. Blanchard inadequately engaged stakeholders in the decision-making process
D. Mr. Blanchard's hiring process is inadequate for his staffing needs

38. **The students at Cornwell Elementary School have consistently surpassed district and state achievement test levels. Prior to the scores being released to the wider school community, the principal receives an internal report and realizes that the scores are in the lower quartile. For the principal, the MOST appropriate first step to take at the school site would be to:**
(Rigorous) (Skill 6.1 A)

A. Meet with the parents to rally their support early in the process
B. Call an emergency faculty meeting to decide what to do
C. Analyze test results to determine areas and patterns of poor performance by students
D. Get assistance from the district supervisor on actions that have worked elsewhere

39. **Which of the following is the best formative assessment practice for classroom instruction?**
(Average) (Skill 6.2)

A. Provide a comprehensive multiple choice test at the end of the chapter
B. Provide several teacher-made quizzes while the chapter is being taught
C. Provide guided practice during the unit
D. Provide a combination of test formats in the end-of-chapter test

40. **What is the best example of a summative assessment?**
(Easy) (Skill 6.2)

A. The results of an intelligence test
B. Correcting tests in small groups and immediately recording the grades
C. An essay that is assigned and graded at the end of the quarter
D. Scheduling a discussion prior to a test

41. **Which of the following is the LEAST appropriate reason for teachers to analyze data on their students?**
(Easy) (Skill 6.2)

A. To separate students into weaker and stronger academic groups
B. To make instructional decisions
C. To provide appropriate instruction
D. To communicate and determine instructional progress

42. **In _____ , school-wide efforts and work tasks are completed in teams.**
(Easy) (Skill 6.4 A)

A. professional learning communities
B. professional lesson cooperatives
C. professional development triads
D. None of the above

DOMAIN III MANAGING ORGANIZATIONAL SYSTEMS AND SAFETY

43. **Which of the following statement(s) describe(s) the responsibilities of today's principals?**
(Easy) (Skill 7.1)

A. A principal is responsible for ensuring that the operational system functions at its highest, most effective level
B. A principal must resolve conflict in a systematic, fair manner and promote this behavior in others
C. A principal is responsible for maintaining a positive perception of the school and must control negative information about all aspects of the school
D. All of the above

44. **The _____ is used for the day-to-day operation of the school.**
(Easy) (Skill 8.1 A)

A. internal services fund
B. general fund
C. debt-services fund
D. special revenues fund

45. Which of the following accounts are used by school principals to encourage and recognize learning achievements?
(Easy) (Skill 8.1 A)

A. PTA account
B. Student activity account
C. Employee benefits account
D. Instructional staff account

46. The district financial officer wants to discuss a fund that has to be used for specific types of expenditures. He is referencing

_____ .
(Average) (Skill 8.1 A)

A. a group of accounts
B. a sum of money
C. a cash balance
D. a ledger

47. A school needs a full-time reading specialist; however, the applicant pool is small and no applicant meets all position requirements. The principal should:
(Average) (Skill 8.2)

A. Select the best person and provide him or her with support
B. Leave the position unfilled and advertise the position again
C. Reassign teachers to cover the position during their planning periods
D. Inform parents that reading will not be taught until a qualified person is hired

48. As chair of a personnel committee considering applicants for an administrative position in the central office, one member of the committee advises you that the superintendent has expressed difficulty in working with female administrators. What action should you take?
(Average) (Skill 8.2)

A. Advise the committee member to introduce this consideration into the committee's deliberations
B. Advise the committee member that the superintendent's expressed difficulty in working with women should be shared in the selection process
C. Suggest a list of questions to be asked of female candidates. These will allow each woman to show the likelihood that she and the superintendent will not have conflicting management styles.
D. Advise the committee member that consideration of the superintendent's expressed difficulty in working with women should not influence the selection of an applicant

49. Why has society come to view principals not simply as managers but as instructional leaders?
(Rigorous) (Skill 8.3)

A. Today's principals need to focus on making sure the building is running smoothly
B. Today's principals can now stay in their offices and delegate teaching activities to others
C. Principals are now required to guide teachers in providing high learning outcomes for all students
D. Principals do not need to focus on what is occurring in individual classrooms; rather, they must focus on school-wide matters such as managing school budgets

50. An appropriate district-level orientation activity for a group of new teachers is
(Easy) (Skill 8.4)

A. To discuss the philosophies of the highest performing schools in the district
B. To introduce them to the senior staff who are shared between schools in the district
C. To review the district's policy manual
D. All of the above

51. In performance-based assessments the principal ties teachers' performance to:
(Easy) (Skill 8.4)

A. Student learning
B. Parental feedback
C. Administrative ratings
D. Student surveys

52. An employee has been incompetent all year although you have followed all steps to help her. She has instituted a grievance against you for allegedly harassing her and claims that she is an excellent teacher as demonstrated by her work at other schools. You have documented her work and through the grapevine you learn that she was under personal stress but has recently resolved these issues. What should you do to decide her fate for the upcoming school year?
(Average) (Skill 8.4)

A. Terminate her
B. Discuss the matter with another principal
C. Rehire her because her performance was affected by personal problems that will no longer hinder her performance
D. Evaluate her against the district's pre-selected criteria

53. A news exposé showed pictures of Monroe High School with missing ceiling tiles, broken toilets, and emergency doors that were jammed. The principal was supposedly unaware of these issues before the story aired. Which of the following is the most effective strategy for a principal to avoid falling into a similar embarrassing situation? *(Rigorous) (Skill 9.1)*

   A. Recognizing that the physical environment must be a top priority for the principal to oversee, perhaps by shifting his/her focus from overseeing instructional matters
   B. Encouraging the students and staff to report issues
   C. Using a checklist to review the physical environment, and if necessary, delegating the task to ensure that this check is performed routinely
   D. All of the above

54. The opposite of an evacuation plan is a _____ plan. *(Easy) (Skill 9.1)*

   A. closed-campus
   B. panic-mode
   C. security-precaution
   D. lock-down

55. Which of the following is an appropriate procedure for dealing with students who misbehave on a regular basis? *(Easy) (Skill 9.3)*

   A. Use modeling and coaching for students to learn appropriate behaviors
   B. Trust that the students will behave and allow them freedom
   C. Allow enough time so that while students transition from one class to another they can have down time
   D. Use verbal private reprimands

DOMAIN IV COLLABORATING WITH KEY STAKEHOLDERS

56. Principals should seek to engage parents in the school's efforts. Which of the following is the greatest reason for involving parents? *(Easy) (Skill 10.1)*

   A. Because parents share a common desire for their children to do well
   B. Because some parents had negative experiences when they were in school
   C. Because some parents were star pupils
   D. Because parents usually have little effect on a school's plans

57. Why must administrators ensure that outside agencies are involved in the operation of schools?
(Average) (Skill 10.1)

A. Students should be able to see how community organizations are interrelated

B. This helps students see that what they learn in school is connected to real life

C. Field trips and guest speakers help keep learning exciting

D. All of the above

58. Last year School Y was on the state's list of critically low-performing schools. No measurable gains were recorded during the second year and consequently, the school is on the list for two years in-a-row. Which of the following is the best strategy to support turn-around efforts?
(Rigorous) (Skill 10.1)

A. Involve the community to identify other schools that have been working to increase their performance.

B. Have a meeting with teachers and establish a strategic plan that focuses on increasing parental involvement in the school.

C. Secure advice from the state and district and work on the problem.

D. Create a committee of teachers, parents, students, and community members to obtain information and to develop a plan of action.

59. Your high school's drama academy recently won first-place honors at the State Thespian Festival. Which of these actions would BEST serve to engage the parents and community members who live near your school?
(Average) (Skill 10.1 B)

A. Schedule a free "open to the public" event at which students present their winning vignettes

B. Write an article for a nationally-recognized educational journal

C. Hold a news conference for the local newspaper, radio, and television organizations

D. Display the award on the activities board in front of the school

60. **As the superintendent, you would like to propose that additional income be raised through an increase in property taxes. Why should a public relations campaign be utilized during this process?**
(Average) (Skill 10.5 A)

A. To create a proposal that will highlight the benefits of the increase

B. To analyze and address the opinions, emotions, and interests of different community groups

C. To create a commercial that will be broadcast on the television station watched by most parents in the district

D. To collect data from the community that can be presented to the Board of Education

61. **Because schools are open systems and operate within a community environment, a school with an effective community relations program and a positive image may be more effective in:**
(Easy) (Skill 10.5 A)

A. Obtaining federal grants to support school programs

B. Securing support from the community to carry out projects

C. Being selected to appear on television commercials

D. Sending more of its graduates off to college

62. **Recommended practice suggests that which of the following should be involved in the decision-making process concerning school improvement?**
(Easy) (Skill 11.1)

I. Teachers
II. Community Partners
III. Administrators
IV. Parents and students

A. I and III only
B. II and III only
C. I, III, and IV only
D. I, II, III, and IV

63. **When using site-based management, why should a principal involve a diverse group of stakeholders in the planning and decision-making processes?**
(Rigorous) (Skill 11.3)

A. The Civil Rights Act requires that diverse groups participate in all parts of school management

B. It avoids conflict when choices are made because every person is represented by individuals on the committee

C. A committee of diverse individuals cannot represent everyone; however, they are more likely to bring different perspectives compared to a non-diverse committee

D. This guarantees that special-interest groups will not have grounds on which to bring legal action against the school

64. **Ms. Martinez teaches World Geography at a high school where 60% of the students are Hispanic, 25% are African American, and 15% are European American. If she wants to benefit from the diversity of her students at the start the school year, which of the following would be the best project for her to assign?** *(Rigorous) (Skill 11.4)*

A. Give each student a map of the world on which to identify and color a list of countries; she would then display the maps.

B. Have each student locate his or her family's country(ies) or continent(s) of origin on a large world map. Then have students share their families' histories outside of and/or within the United States.

C. Have students work in homogeneous groups and compare the similarities and differences of their parents' families.

D. Give an overview of the semester's objectives; assign the first chapter of the textbook and have students work in groups to compare their answers to the questions at the end of the chapter.

65. **When assessments incorporate cultural knowledge, history, experiences, and relevance of contextual knowledge, they are:** *(Easy) (Skill 11.4)*

A. Traditionally-focused
B. Knowledge-based
C. Culturally-responsive
D. All of the above

66. **Keeping the campus safe and welcoming for all students is a _____ issue** *(Easy) (Skill 11.4)*

A. cognitive
B. sociological
C. linguistic
D. cultural

67. **A principal learns that the district is requiring each school to have a coordinated technology plan. The directive requires that each week, each class uses the mobile technology lab to enhance learning. Identify the most cost-effective method to meet this need:**
(Rigorous) (Skill 12.3 A)

   A. Analyzing the school schedule and appointing two team members who have a morning and an afternoon time slot to reallocate to this task
   B. Selecting members of the student council who have already taken all their prerequisites and who have open slots in their schedules
   C. Hiring a new staff member on a one year position approved by the teachers' union
   D. Placing the laptops in an unused classroom and allowing teachers to bring their classes to the lab bi-weekly

68. **To reduce the chances of alienating the audience, a speaker must:**
(Average) (Skill 12.4)

   A. Plan an in-depth report of facts and statistics to support his or her argument
   B. Analyze his or her biases, emotions, and interests so they do not alter the message
   C. Make an impassioned, emotional appeal
   D. Solicit listener opinions after stating the objective

69. **Principal Brown has recently begun attending the local senior citizens' council meeting. In the short-term, the school can likely benefit from this relationship by:**
(Easy) (Skill 12.4)

   A. Asking the group to fund a new addition to the school
   B. Engaging members as reading volunteers
   C. Having the organization lobby the city council on the school's behalf
   D. None of the above

70. **There are six phases of communication: ideating, encoding, transmitting, receiving, decoding, and acting. Which of the following includes one phase that involves the sender and one phase that involves the receiver?**
(Rigorous) (Skill 12.4 A)

   A. Ideating and encoding
   B. Receiving and decoding
   C. Ideating and decoding
   D. None of the above

DOMAIN V ETHICS AND INTEGRITY

71. **Why is a code of conduct an important document?**
(Average) (Skill 13.1 B)

   A. It identifies a committee that can be called upon if a situation arises and the code itself cannot provide adequate guidance.
   B. To provide a litmus test for behaviors
   C. It identifies pre-determined consequences for violators
   D. All of the above

72. A federal law that governs the disclosure of student education records is:
(Easy) (Skill 13.2)

A. HERPA
B. FERPA
C. FREPA
D. HEFPA

73. Electronic files and computerized databases are kept secure by which of the following groups in the technology team?
(Average) (Skill 13.2)

A. Network
B. Hardware
C. Peripheral
D. CAI

74. To prepare students to be good citizens, the principal should do which of the following?
(Rigorous) (Skill 13.3)

A. Encourage students to seek out role models who have achieved success in business
B. Foster an environment that emphasizes ethical principles, moral values, and civic participation
C. Encourage students to rethink cultural practices that are opposed to the norms and practices of the larger society
D. All of the above

75. A principal can serve as an ambassador by doing all of the following EXCEPT:
(Average) (Skill 13.3)

A. Attending community events
B. Participating in meetings held by local groups
C. Joining important civic organizations
D. Serving as the school arbitrator for district-wide staff disputes

76. Many people believe that a great educational system is necessary for a thriving society because:
(Easy) (Skill 13.3)

A. It fuels economic growth
B. It fosters societal development
C. It focuses communities on preparing its children for productive citizenship
D. All of the above

77. When an educational leader values each individual he or she will be:
(Easy) (Skill 14.1)

A. Traditionally-focused
B. Knowledge-based
C. Culturally-responsive
D. Historically accurate

78. **Which of the following is a strategy to foster a respectful and inclusive environment?**
(Easy) (Skill 14.1)

   A. Creating a system of rewards and recognition
   B. Developing effective teams
   C. Establishing trust
   D. All of the above

79. **In the organizational development approach, each person must feel that he or she has the autonomy to contribute something of value to the team. Autonomy comes from the key value of:**
(Easy) (Skill 14.1)

   A. Empowerment
   B. Collaboration
   C. Authenticity
   D. Respect and inclusion

80. **According to Galpin and Whittington, which of the following is NOT a ground rule that encourages authenticity and honesty?**
(Average) (Skill 14.4 A)

   A. Staying on the current topic
   B. Participating in the discussion as often as possible
   C. Agreeing to disagree if consensus can't be reached
   D. Using active listening, including reading non-verbal language

81. **According to the Society for Organizational Learning (SoL), making your thinking and reasoning more visible to others is called _____.**
(Average) (Skill 14.4 A)

   A. Reflection
   B. Inquiry
   C. Advocacy
   D. None of the above

82. **If a school has been identified as low-performing for the first year, the state may require that the School Improvement Plan include:**
(Average) (Skill 15.1 A)

   A. Parent contracts for all students in the school
   B. Collective bargaining for all employees
   C. A plan for all administrators to engage in leadership-based professional development
   D. A take-over plan

83. **During times of crisis the principal can help the school stay on course by:**
(Rigorous) (Skill 15.4)

   A. Talking about the crisis in the past tense so everyone remembers the situation is only temporary
   B. Keeping the vision and goals in the forefront of everyone's mind so the situation does not divert the school from its charted course
   C. Implementing an intensive long-term solution so that the team can work on the issue in segments
   D. Making sure that full energies are devoted toward the crisis so that it can be handled as quickly as possible

84. **The _____ determines the longevity of the proposed solution and the probable recurrence of the same or similar difficulties.**
(Average) (Skill 15.4 A)

   A. quality of the problem-solving strategy
   B. principal's ability to engage external stakeholders
   C. level of communication with faculty members
   D. ability to raise the necessary funds

DOMAIN VI THE EDUCATIONAL SYSTEM

85. **The U.S. Department of Education has recently updated the Elementary and Secondary Education Act (ESEA). In three years it will require the state to implement a new assessment that all students must master in order for them to graduate from high school. In the first month after the policy is announced, what is the best strategy to prepare parents for its implementation?**
(Average) (Skill 16.1 A)

   A. Post basic information on a bulletin board so parents can learn about the new policy
   B. Call all parents so they are aware of the change and can make immediate preparations for their children who will have to take the assessment
   C. Plan a pep rally for students in the neighborhood middle school so they are aware of the assessment they will need to take
   D. All of the above

86. The school's boilers stopped working on Friday night and the school does not have a mass-calling system. Which method of communication is the most considerate, efficient, and cost-effective to inform parents that the school will be closed?
(Rigorous) (Skill 16.1 B)

A. Post a sign on the doors so parents know why the building is not open when they come to drop off the children
B. Send an email to all parents and ask that they respond confirming receipt. Then a plan can be created for parents who may not have received the information
C. Ask each teacher to call the homes of his/her first period students
D. None of the above

87. The acronym FAQ stands for:
(Easy) (Skill 16.1 B)

A. Faculty Area Questionnaire
B. Frequently Asked Questions
C. Faculty Assistance Questions
D. Frequently Assessed Questionnaire

88. To facilitate discussion-oriented, non-threatening communication, administrators must do which of the following:
(Average) (Skill 16.1 B)

A. Model appropriate behavior
B. Allow other stakeholders to express themselves freely
C. Explain that parents, teachers, and administrators are all working for the good of students and therefore, they should not disagree
D. All of the above

89. Administrators should network with other stakeholders for all of the following reasons EXCEPT _____?
(Easy) (Skill 16.2)

A. To discuss challenges facing schools, teachers, and education in general
B. To develop a sense of community
C. To fulfill the necessary requirements for licensure renewal
D. To find solutions to difficult problems

90. Often, schools and communities interact for the following activities EXCEPT?
(Easy) (Skill 16.2)

A. Blood drives
B. Legal proceedings
C. Meeting room use
D. Elections

91. When embracing diversity, educators must ensure that they neither protect students from criticism nor praise them because of their ethnicity or gender. Doing either action may result in which of the following outcomes?
(Easy) (Skill 16.3)

   A. Classmates may become anxious or resentful when dealing with the diverse students
   B. Parents will appreciate their child being singled out
   C. The child will be pleased to receive this attention
   D. Other teachers will follow this example

92. Of the following definitions, which best describes an evidence-based approach to academic planning?
(Rigorous) (Skill 17.1)

   A. It focuses on narrow skills and abilities
   B. It relies on assessment data to define the school's strengths and weaknesses
   C. It focuses on federal, state, and local standards
   D. It measures test performance related to specific, recently acquired information

93. Administrators must hold themselves to high standards. When they engage in negative actions such as fighting with parents, they are violating all of the following EXCEPT:
(Easy) (Skill 17.2)

   A. Ethics
   B. Professionalism
   C. Morals
   D. Fiscal responsibility

94. Instructional design teams plan more effectively for instruction when they:
(Average) (Skill 17.3)

   A. Describe the role of the teacher and student
   B. Rearrange the order of activities
   C. Assess the outcomes of prior instruction
   D. All of the above

95. **Mr. Rogers describes his educational philosophy as eclectic, meaning that he uses many educational theories to guide his classroom practice. Why is this strategy the best approach for today's teachers?** *(Rigorous) (Skill 17.3)*

    A. Today's classrooms are often too diverse for one theory to meet the needs of all students

    B. If one theory is not effective educators must be able to draw upon other strategies

    C. This allows the teacher to select from a variety of methods rather than being limited to one school of thought or practice

    D. All of the above

ANSWER KEY

1. A	33. A	65. C
2. C	34. D	66. B
3. A	35. C	67. A
4. C	36. B	68. B
5. D	37. C	69. B
6. A	38. C	70. C
7. C	39. B	71. D
8. D	40. C	72. B
9. C	41. A	73. A
10. B	42. A	74. B
11. B	43. D	75. D
12. A	44. B	76. D
13. B	45. B	77. C
14. D	46. A	78. D
15. B	47. A	79. A
16. A	48. D	80. B
17. C	49. C	81. C
18. B	50. C	82. C
19. D	51. A	83. B
20. C	52. D	84. A
21. B	53. C	85. A
22. B	54. D	86. B
23. B	55. A	87. B
24. B	56. A	88. A
25. C	57. D	89. C
26. A	58. D	90. B
27. B	59. A	91. A
28. D	60. B	92. B
29. D	61. B	93. D
30. B	62. D	94. C
31. A	63. C	95. D
32. B	64. B	

SAMPLE TEST WITH RATIONALES

DOMAIN I VISION AND GOALS

1.   **An example of reliability in testing is:**
     (Average) (Skill 1.1 B)

     A.   Items on the test produce the same response each time
     B.   The test was administered with poor lighting
     C.   Items on the test measure what they should measure
     D.   The test is too long for the time allotted

Answer: A. Items on the test produce the same response each time
When a test is reliable, it produces the same response each time. A test should give the same results when administered under the same conditions and to the same types of students. This will occur only when the items on the test are clear, unambiguous, and not confusing for the students. When items on the test measure what they should measure, this is called validity.

2.   **_____ is a standardized test in which performance is directly related to the educational objective(s)**
     (Average) (Skill 1.1 B)

     A.   An aptitude test
     B.   A norm-referenced test
     C.   A criterion-referenced test
     D.   A summative evaluation

Answer: C. A criterion-referenced test
A criterion-referenced test takes the educational objectives of a course and rewrites them in the form of questions. The questions on the test are directly related to the objectives upon which the instruction is based. Thus the results of a criterion-referenced test will indicate which objectives of the course a student has mastered and which ones he or she has not mastered.

3.   Fill in the blanks for I. _____ and II. _____ in the picture below:
      (Rigorous) (Skill 1.1 B)

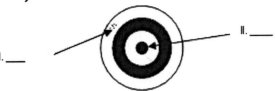

      A.   I. Reliability and II. Validity
      B.   I. Validity and II. Reliability
      C.   I. Reliability and II. Vigor
      D.   I. Rigor and II. Validity

Answer: A. I. Reliability and II. Validity
This picture represents I. Reliability and II. Validity. An assessment has validity if the dart hits the target. There is reliability if the same spot is hit time after time. The goal should be to develop assessments that are both valid and reliable.

4.   **Your district is considering implementing block scheduling in each of its high schools. As principal of one of these schools and a strong advocate of block scheduling, your best approach to involving the faculty in the decision-making process is to:**
      (Easy) (Skill 1.2)

      A.   Present only the advantages of block scheduling
      B.   Present and invalidate all objections to block scheduling
      C.   Present advantages and objections, relating each to the school's vision
      D.   Present the school board position as inevitable and seek the best methods of implementing block scheduling at your school site

Answer: C. Present advantages and objections, relating each to the school's vision
This approach will receive more credibility, since the principal will not be turning a blind eye to the objections.

5. **When implementing the selected vision and goals, the school leader must make sure they are aligned with:**
    (Average) (Skill 1.2 A)

    A. Federal research
    B. Community town-hall meetings
    C. Student proposals
    D. State and district standards or requirements

Answer: D. State and district standards or requirements
To implement the selected vision and goals, the principal must make sure they are aligned with state and district standards and federal mandates for student learning.

6. **Goals are often drafted using the SMART method. Which one of the following is NOT a component of this acronym?**
    (Average) (Skill 1.2 C)

    A. Scorable
    B. Relevant
    C. Achievable
    D. Time-framed

Answer: A. Scorable
The SMART method suggests that goals should be: S – specific, M – measurable, A – achievable, R – relevant, and T- time-framed.

7. **At a community roundtable convened by the principal, business leaders expressed concern that they have been unable to hire recent graduates. They cite a lack of technological knowledge as the main reason why jobs could not be offered to the school's former students. The administration was able to identify this gap because they:**
    (Easy) (Skill 2.1)

    A. Researched the Census Bureau's employment data
    B. Continued to engage students on Facebook™
    C. Engaged parents and other stakeholders from the community
    D. Administered surveys about the jobs held by parents

Answer: C. Engaged parents and other stakeholders from the community
Through parent nights and advisory committees, the administration and faculty have opportunities to learn about the community's perception of the school and issues that might have an impact on the school's progress.

8. The district has adopted a new grading scale that is stricter than the state requirement. Which of the following would be the most <u>time-efficient</u> means of obtaining feedback from the community?
    (Easy) (Skill 2.4)

    A. Distributing an end-of-year school improvement survey
    B. Holding meetings with small groups of parent volunteers
    C. Delivering a presentation at a school board meeting
    D. Participating in an interview on a popular local radio station with responses to questions called in by listeners

Answer: D. Participating in an interview on a popular local radio station with responses to questions called in by listeners
This would allow specific concerns to be discussed and give community members a chance to be directly involved in the process, whether as listeners or as call-in guests. The school can also use specific strategies to notify constituents who do not normally listen to the radio. The event should be promoted with signs around the school and with emails to parents and other key constituents.

9. Communication in which a school principal receives feedback from the faculty/staff is:
    (Easy) (Skill 2.4 A)

    A. Downward
    B. Lateral
    C. Upward
    D. Diagonal

Answer: C. Upward
Upward communication happens when personnel share information with a supervisor.

10. **Which of the following represents the proper sequential order in the communication process?**
(Easy) (Skill 2.4 A)

   A. Ideating, decoding, transmitting, receiving, encoding, acting
   B. Ideating, encoding, transmitting, receiving, decoding, acting
   C. Ideating, transmitting, encoding, receiving, decoding, acting
   D. Ideating, encoding, transmitting, receiving, acting, decoding

Answer: B. Ideating, encoding, transmitting, receiving, decoding, acting
The six steps of communication are:

- **Ideating**: Development of idea or message to be communicated
- **Encoding**: Organization of idea into conveyable symbols
- **Transmitting**: Delivery of message through a medium
- **Receiving**: Claiming of message by receiver
- **Decoding**: Translation of message by receiver
- **Acting**: Action taken by receiver in response to message

11. **The administration drafts the master plan of teaching assignments for the coming school year. This step will most likely increase teacher commitment to the vision and goal:**
(Easy) (Skill 2.5)

   A. If the plan is finalized in time to notify teachers of their assignments before the end of the current school year
   B. If some teachers are members of the planning committee and if all teachers are able to provide input toward the final plan
   C. Even if last-minute changes have to be made before school opens
   D. Because they know that the administration is acting in good faith

Answer: B. If some teachers are members of the planning committee and if all teachers are able to provide input toward the final plan
Soliciting teacher feedback will boost their morale. It will show that the administration respects and includes them in important decisions. By having some teachers work on the committee, the faculty's voices will be heard during the planning phase. Later, when the final plans are being made, all teachers will be able to give their feedback in ways that are useful and productive to completing the schedule.

12. In defining the _____ model, key values include respect and inclusion, collaboration, authenticity, and self-awareness
(Average) (Skill 2.5)

    A.   organizational development
    B.   theory of change
    C.   practitioner's guide
    D.   leadership initiative

Answer: A. organizational development
In the organizational development model, key values include respect and inclusion, collaboration, authenticity, self-awareness, and empowerment.

13. Conducting _____ is the process of gathering information to identify and define the problem before initiating a project or program.
(Rigorous) (Skill 3.1)

    A.   a survey
    B.   a needs assessment
    C.   an evaluation
    D.   None of the above

Answer: B. a needs assessment
A needs assessment is a wise first step in program or curriculum planning. It provides the opportunity to survey stakeholders and identify the context in which the program will be developed. The needs assessment should focus primarily on the needs of the students.

14. When the administration is working to achieve the vision and goals of the school, which of the following strategies should they use?
(Average) (Skill 3.2)

    A.   Analyze data specific to their school
    B.   Read current educational research
    C.   Visit a school that exemplifies the high test scores and vision of NCLB
    D.   All of the above

Answer: D. All of the Above
To achieve the vision and goals of the school, the administration should engage in decision-making processes that are guided by school-based data, current educational research, and knowledge of best practices that can be emulated. Such practices can be observed by visiting schools that demonstrate high standardized test scores and that exemplify the vision of NCLB.

15. **Which of the following is a more LONG-TERM reason for teachers to facilitate productive, eager learners?**
(Rigorous) (Skill 3.2)

    A.   These students cause fewer disruptions than students who are bored
    B.   These students apply new knowledge in class and in their life experiences
    C.   These students usually come from wealthier, more affluent families
    D.   All of the above

Answer: B. These students apply new knowledge in class and in their life experiences
Effective teachers facilitate productive learners who love learning and are eager to apply new knowledge in the classroom and in their life experiences.

16. **Some critics suggest that the original form of No Child Left Behind (NCLB) relied on external rather than internal motivation. What argument is used to support this position?**
(Rigorous) (Skill 3.3)

    A.   It relied on the principle that rewards and punishments would increase motivational levels of teachers, principals, and students
    B.   It utilized incremental growth targets that were more intrinsic than extrinsic
    C.   The 2010 refinement of NCLB provides rewards for outstanding teachers and leaders
    D.   It sought to harness the external mechanisms that cause individuals to achieve, grow and develop, and reach their potential

Answer: A. It relied on the principle that rewards and punishments would increase motivational levels of teachers, principals, and students
The term "educational accountability" sometimes means that educational policies rely on the idea of external motivation to improve instructional quality. In its original form NCLB operated largely on the principle that rewards and punishments would increase motivational levels of teachers, principals, and students.

17. At times, administrators must force teachers to change. What should a school principal do to help teachers adapt to forced change?
(Rigorous) (Skill 3.4)

    A. Require teachers to adapt to changes quickly and with minimal negativity
    B. Present all the changes together; this helps to engage in all change-acceptance processes at the same time
    C. Gather data to help teachers make sense of why changes are necessary
    D. Adhere to the dictates of a collegial environment; this may mean rejecting the change if the teachers are not in favor of it

Answer: C. Gather data to help teachers make sense of why changes are necessary
There will be times when teachers must be forced to change. The administrator has to realize that some strategies can help facilitate these changes. An important one is gathering data to give meaning to the change(s). By involving all stakeholders in the early phases of program reform, it is easier to gain buy-in and support for the changes that need to be made.

18. Informal lateral communication does all of the following EXCEPT:
(Average) (Skill 3.6 A)

    A. Serves as a vehicle for peer-to-peer communication
    B. Provides a hierarchy through which information is distributed
    C. Becomes a means of cohesion for team members
    D. Facilitates sharing information quickly

Answer: B. Provides a hierarchy through which information is distributed
Informal lateral communication does not involve the traditional, hierarchical, top-down approach to communication.

DOMAIN II TEACHING AND LEARNING

19.   **When preparing for individualized classroom instruction, which of the following strategies should be used?**
      (Rigorous) (Skill 4.1 C)

      A.   Give the same level of instruction to all students so that the same content is presented to everyone
      B.   Exempt certain children whose special-needs conditions would reduce their ability to understand the content
      C.   Provide a lengthier test period for the entire class to complete standardized assessments (i.e., provide everyone with four hours instead of three or two)
      D.   None of the above

Answer: D. None of the above
The intent of individualizing instruction and assessment is to provide all students with the opportunity to learn the content and achieve to their full potential. To reduce learning gaps, teachers must be supported in applying multiple methods of assessment and instruction. By individualizing classroom instruction, every child will have appropriate opportunities to master the subject matter, demonstrate such mastery, and improve and enhance learning skills with each lesson.

20.   **Which of the following is MOST LIKELY to assist participants in staff development activities to retain information?**
      (Easy) (Skill 4.2)

      A.   Cover the topic in a single-session workshop
      B.   Cover the topic in a three-to-four-session workshop
      C.   Cover the topic throughout the school year, allowing teachers to try the strategies, and then report back
      D.   Cover the topic daily at informal meetings

Answer: C. Cover the topic throughout the school year, allowing teachers to try the strategies, and then report back
The new model of staff development focuses on sustaining learning. Instead of providing teachers with a single training session, the topic is brought up throughout a school year. This might, for example, allow teachers to learn the strategy at the beginning of the year and try it for a few months before reporting back and working toward refining the strategy.

21. **Which of the following is the LEAST effective model of professional development?**
(Average) (Skill 4.2)

   A. Workshops held once per month which focus on the same topic for three months at a time
   B. An intensive one-day workshop with specific activities for teachers to implement in their classrooms
   C. Ongoing planning meetings to adapt new materials to the school
   D. Classroom assistance by resource personnel to assist with program implementation over time

Answer: B. An intensive one-day workshop with specific activities for teachers to implement in their classrooms
A single day workshop will do very little to provide the professional support and development teachers need for new programs or ideas. The professional development needs to be continuous and monitored so that it too can change as needed. Items A, C, and D should all be used in combination with one another to provide the most support for teachers.

22. **Between the two methods of motivation:**
(Average) (Skill 4.2 A)

   A. Extrinsic motivation is better; it is easy to find rewards to get teachers to perform
   B. Intrinsic motivation is better; teachers want to engage in professional development without needing rewards or punishments
   C. Extrinsic motivation is better; teachers are internally motivated
   D. Intrinsic motivation is better; teachers try to avoid punishments

Answer: B. Intrinsic motivation is better; teachers want to engage in professional development without needing rewards or punishments
Intrinsic motivation is when a person is motivated by internal, as opposed to external, factors. Intrinsic motivation drives a person to do things because the individual believes these things are fun or are a good or right thing to do. Intrinsic motivation is a much stronger motivator than extrinsic motivation.

23. To encourage a school environment that embraces change, the educational leader should do all of the following EXCEPT:
(Average) (Skill 4.3)

   A. Model openness to change
   B. Commit to using democratic processes to make all decisions
   C. Collaborate with stakeholders to discuss the need for change
   D. Demonstrate a willingness to change own position on an issue

Answer: B. Commit to using democratic processes to make all decisions
The educational leader will not be able to use the democratic process to make all decisions.

24. Select the statement that best describes the table below.
(Rigorous) (Skill 4.4 A)

	High Relationship	Low Relationship
High Task Behavior	Organizational Mode	Crisis Mode
Low Task Behavior	Interpersonal Mode	Routine Mode

   A. This table shows the four modes or strategies for developing individual goals
   B. This table describes the four group problem-solving modes in situational leadership
   C. This table is a replication of Fiedler's four-stage contingency theory
   D. This table depicts the major steps in developing an MBO program

Answer: B. This table describes the four group problem-solving modes in situational leadership
When using the situational leadership quadrants, there is an effort to move from the routine mode to the organizational mode. This is an evolution from traditional educational leadership in which administrators focused on crisis mode that has low relationships and high task behavior.

25.	To encourage team-teaching, the administration should do which of the following:
	(Average) (Skill 4.4 B)

	A.	Pair teachers by subject area rather than by grade level
	B.	Pair teachers by grade level rather than by subject area
	C.	Schedule the day so teachers have their prep periods at the same time
	D.	Schedule teachers to work in teams for a week-at-a-time

Answer: C. Schedule the day so teachers have their prep periods at the same time
To encourage team-teaching, the administration should schedule the day so teachers have their prep periods at the same time. Teams can be paired by subject area or by grade level. However, teams should work together for an ongoing basis, not simply for a week-at-a-time.

26.	In _____ there is the belief that "the more power we share, the more power we have to use".
	(Easy) (Skill 4.5)

	A.	collaborative leadership
	B.	democratic leadership
	C.	creative leadership
	D.	All of the above

Answer: A. collaborative leadership
According to the Leadership Development National Excellence Collaborative, "collaborative leadership requires a new notion of power...the more power we share, the more power we have to use."

27.	Which of the following is a strategy to individualize instruction and make the student responsible for his or her own learning?
	(Easy) (Skill 4.6 A)

	A.	A lesson plan
	B.	A learning contract
	C.	An administrative directive
	D.	A student study plan

Answer: B. A learning contract
A learning contract is a way of individualizing instruction and making the student responsible for his or her own learning. In the contract method, the student can progress at his or her own pace and learn at the rate he or she needs in order to achieve the stated learning outcomes.

28. **Administrators who engage in scholastic writing to share effective educational strategies are coveted in school districts. Why?**
(Rigorous) (Skill 4.7)

   A. It is important that administrators be able to communicate with others about effective strategies
   B. Administrators need time to reflect on their practice and scholastic writing is one way to present new paradigms and theoretical constructs
   C. To share effective educational strategies, the administrator must be aware, and likely utilize, best practices
   D. All of the above

Answer: D. All of the above
When administrators can engage in scholastic writing to share effective educational strategies, they are coveted in school districts. These individuals have the ability to present new paradigms, theoretical constructs of leadership, and educational best practices. By engaging in the publication process they share effective strategies and also take time to reflect on their practice.

29. **After three years of implementing its School Improvement Plan, School Five has learned that over 90% of its students mastered the mandated state standards and have performed at the proficient level on the state-required assessment. This is likely a result of:**
(Easy) (Skill 5.1)

   A. Shadowing a school in a neighboring state
   B. Focusing on research regarding future trends in math and reading
   C. Engaging parents to provide extracurricular enrichment activities
   D. Creating a school-wide commitment to standards-based instruction

Answer: D. Creating a school-wide commitment to standards-based instruction
Students need to master the mandated state standards and perform well on state-required assessments. This can happen when administrators create a school-wide commitment to standards-based instruction.

30. **A school-based instructional team is developing learning objectives. Which of the following lists the top two areas they should consider?**
(Average) (Skill 5.1)

  A.   Textbooks and bibliographies
  B.   State-standards and students
  C.   Teachers and administrators
  D.   Parents and community groups

Answer: B. State-standards and students
High-level objectives have to meet or exceed state standards and be established for individual classes and the building as a whole. The instructional team must consider students at various developmental-levels and create a program that meets the needs of students at each level.

31. **Which of the following best illustrates an observable objective?**
(Average) (Skill 5.1)

  A.   Eighty percent of students will be able to solve multiplication word problems at the rate of one problem per minute with 75 percent accuracy
  B.   Students will appreciate the originality of cultural music
  C.   Ten percent of the students will comprehend the implications of good health and physical fitness
  D.   All of the above

Answer: A. Eighty percent of students will be able to solve multiplication word problems at the rate of one problem per minute with 75 percent accuracy
Objectives of lessons are stated in terms of observable behaviors. In that way all stakeholders including administrators, teachers, students, and parents know what kind of behavior they expect to see in student performance. The main part of an objective is the verb, which is usually expressed in terms of what the student will be able to do at the end of instruction. The objective should be specific and measurable.

32.   **The best way to improve a school is to:**
       (Easy) (Skill 5.1 C)

    A.   Obtain a nationally recognized authority on the topic
    B.   Involve teachers in initiating, planning, implementing, and evaluating the program
    C.   Have teachers advertise the program
    D.   Have the principal plan and let a few teachers review the plan

Answer: B. Involve teachers in initiating, planning, implementing, and evaluating the program
Involving more teachers in all phases of the program will increase accountability and feelings of ownership. This will promote greater success.

33.   _____ **reviews the program environment and its met and unmet needs.**
       (Average) (Skill 5.3)

    A.   Content evaluation
    B.   Input evaluation
    C.   Process evaluation
    D.   Product evaluation

Answer: A. Content evaluation
A content evaluation reviews the program environment and its met and unmet needs.

34.   **Which of the following refers to the horizontal organization of the elements of the curriculum?**
       (Rigorous) (Skill 5.4 A)

    A.   The knowledge and skills students learn are useful in life situations
    B.   The knowledge and skills that students learn at one grade level are relevant and useful as they progress to other grades
    C.   Everything the student learns contributes to fulfillment
    D.   During a school year, what students learn in one class supports and reinforces what they learn in other classes during that same year

Answer: D. During a school year, what students learn in one class supports and reinforces what they learn in other classes during that same year
Horizontal organization refers to making students aware of how the various subjects of the curriculum are interconnected. Teachers of different subject areas plan together so that they can teach and reinforce the same skills.

35. The annual Campus Improvement Plan (CIP) or School Improvement Plan (SIP) should have all of the following EXCEPT:
(Easy) (Skill 5.5 A)

   A.   The school's goals
   B.   Activities to accomplish the school's goals
   C.   The personnel who monitored the previous school goals
   D.   A timeline for completion of the goals

Answer: C. The personnel who monitored the previous school goals
The annual Campus Improvement Plan (CIP) or School Improvement Plan (SIP) delineates the improvement targets for the school. The CIP lists the school's goals along with activities to accomplish the goals, a timeline for completion, and the personnel currently assigned to monitor goal completion.

36. Teachers may resist integrating technology for all of the following reasons EXCEPT:
(Easy) (Skill 5.6)

   A.   Habit of doing the same things for years
   B.   Training and staff development
   C.   Preserving the status quo
   D.   Belief that the new idea will meld with their current beliefs or practices

Answer: B. Training and staff development
Teachers may resist integrating technology unless time is devoted to training and staff development.

37.   Mr. Blanchard has taken care to match the qualifications of new teachers he hires with school needs and district policies. However, by the end of the first semester, he has received numerous complaints about his new hires. Additionally some community leaders have criticized him for the school-wide changes he has implemented. From the information provided, what is a likely explanation for this criticism?
(Rigorous) (Skill 5.7 B)

A.   The new teachers did not buy into the school mission and vision
B.   Students dislike the school vision and have complained to their parents about how the new teachers promote it
C.   Mr. Blanchard inadequately engaged stakeholders in the decision-making process
D.   Mr. Blanchard's hiring process is inadequate for his staffing needs

Answer: C. Mr. Blanchard inadequately engaged stakeholders in the decision-making process
Resources carry emotional and personal weight for school community members. For this reason, forgetting the political elements of running a school often damages relationships. To minimize conflict and maximize support, it is important to engage stakeholders throughout the decision-making process

38.   The students at Cornwell Elementary School have consistently surpassed district and state achievement test levels. Prior to the scores being released to the wider school community, the principal receives an internal report and realizes that the scores are in the lower quartile. For the principal, the MOST appropriate first step to take at the school site would be to:
(Rigorous) (Skill 6.1 A)

A.   Meet with the parents to rally their support early in the process
B.   Call an emergency faculty meeting to decide what to do
C.   Analyze test results to determine areas and patterns of poor performance by students
D.   Get assistance from the district supervisor on actions that have worked elsewhere

Answer: C. Analyze test results to determine areas and patterns of poor performance by students
Student assessment data should be used to identify targets for campus instructional improvement. Once targets for improvement are identified then the principal can enlist appropriate stakeholders to search for effective and research-based improvement strategies.

39. **Which of the following is the best formative assessment practice for classroom instruction?**
(Average) (Skill 6.2)

    A.   Provide a comprehensive multiple choice test at the end of the chapter
    B.   Provide several teacher-made quizzes while the chapter is being taught
    C.   Provide guided practice during the unit
    D.   Provide a combination of test formats in the end-of-chapter test

Answer: B. Provide several teacher-made quizzes while the chapter is being taught
Formative assessment takes place during the process of teaching a lesson. It can be both formal and informal, with the teacher assigning marks or it could be a simple note in the teacher's grade book. It could also be a note to the student alerting him or her of mistakes to watch for.

40. **What is the best example of a summative assessment?**
(Easy) (Skill 6.2)

    A.   The results of an intelligence test
    B.   Correcting tests in small groups and immediately recording the grades
    C.   An essay that is assigned and graded at the end of the quarter
    D.   Scheduling a discussion prior to a test

Answer: C. An essay that is assigned and graded at the end of the quarter
Summative assessments/evaluations are used to culminate a unit or series of lessons. A grade is recorded for the assignment.

41. **Which of the following is the LEAST appropriate reason for teachers to analyze data on their students?**
(Easy) (Skill 6.2)

    A.   To separate students into weaker and stronger academic groups
    B.   To make instructional decisions
    C.   To provide appropriate instruction
    D.   To communicate and determine instructional progress

Answer: A. To separate students into weaker and stronger academic groups
Especially in today's high stakes environment, it is critical for teachers to have a complete understanding of the process involved in examining student data in order to make instructional decisions. Teachers must be cautious of grouping children in homogeneous versus heterogeneous groups. It may appear to save time to group and work with children of similar abilities; however, it has been shown that children in mixed groups benefit from the diversity within the group.

42. In _____, school-wide efforts and work tasks are completed in teams.
(Easy) (Skill 6.4 A)

A. professional learning communities
B. professional lesson cooperatives
C. professional development triads
D. None of the above

Answer: A. professional learning communities
When schools operate as Professional Learning Communities (PLCs), work is completed in teams. A team of professionals develops lessons and likewise, a team works together to craft, pilot-test, revise, and finalize assessments.

DOMAIN III MANAGING ORGANIZATIONAL SYSTEMS AND SAFETY

43. Which of the following statement(s) describe(s) the responsibilities of today's principals?
(Easy) (Skill 7.1)

A. A principal is responsible for ensuring that the operational system functions at its highest, most effective level
B. A principal must resolve conflict in a systematic, fair manner and promote this behavior in others
C. A principal is responsible for maintaining a positive perception of the school and must control negative information about all aspects of the school
D. All of the above

Answer: D. All of the above
Today's principals face new challenges. They must oversee effective operational systems, manage diverse populations fairly and without bias, and create a positive perception of their school.

44. The _____ is used for the day-to-day operation of the school.
(Easy) (Skill 8.1 A)

A. internal services fund
B. general fund
C. debt-services fund
D. special revenues fund

Answer: B. general fund
The general fund is used for the programs, substitute teachers, and all the supplies needed for the school. It also holds the funds for staff salaries.

45. Which of the following accounts are used by school principals to encourage and recognize learning achievements?
     (Easy) (Skill 8.1 A)

     A. PTA account
     B. Student activity account
     C. Employee benefits account
     D. Instructional staff account

Answer: B. Student activity account
The principal has to ensure that the monies from the student activity account are spent on student learning benefits such as award ribbons and trophies.

46. The district financial officer wants to discuss a fund that has to be used for specific types of expenditures. He is referencing _____ .
     (Average) (Skill 8.1 A)

     A. a group of accounts
     B. a sum of money
     C. a cash balance
     D. a ledger

Answer: A. a group of accounts
The funds or account groups are accounting entities with a self-balancing set of accounts that support specific school activities to attain specific objectives. These funds or accounts can only be used for specified purposes.

47. A school needs a full-time reading specialist; however, the applicant pool is small and no applicant meets all position requirements. The principal should:
     (Average) (Skill 8.2)

     A. Select the best person and provide him or her with support
     B. Leave the position unfilled and advertise the position again
     C. Reassign teachers to cover the position during their planning periods
     D. Inform parents that reading will not be taught until a qualified person is hired

Answer: A. Select the best person and provide him or her with support
It is important to have a certified person in each classroom. However, if time does not allow for a continued search, the principal should hire the best candidate and provide a mentor and additional resources to help the teacher develop skills during his or her first year.

48. As chair of a personnel committee considering applicants for an administrative position in the central office, one member of the committee advises you that the superintendent has expressed difficulty in working with female administrators. What action should you take?
(Average) (Skill 8.2)

   A.   Advise the committee member to introduce this consideration into the committee's deliberations
   B.   Advise the committee member that the superintendent's expressed difficulty in working with women should be shared in the selection process
   C.   Suggest a list of questions to be asked of female candidates. These will allow each woman to show the likelihood that she and the superintendent will not have conflicting management styles.
   D.   Advise the committee member that consideration of the superintendent's expressed difficulty in working with women should not influence the selection of an applicant

Answer: D. Advise the committee member that consideration of the superintendent's expressed difficulty in working with women should not influence the selection of an applicant
A selection committee must use a job-related matrix to evaluate candidates for a position. Each candidate for a position must be asked the same questions and judged by the same criteria.

49. Why has society come to view principals not simply as managers but as instructional leaders?
(Rigorous) (Skill 8.3)

   A.   Today's principals need to focus on making sure the building is running smoothly
   B.   Today's principals can now stay in their offices and delegate teaching activities to others
   C.   Principals are now required to guide teachers in providing high learning outcomes for all students
   D.   Principals do not need to focus on what is occurring in individual classrooms; rather, they must focus on school-wide matters such as managing school budgets

Answer: C. Principals are now required to guide teachers in providing high learning outcomes for all students
Previously, principals functioned like the manager of the school building; they made sure that everything was working together according to specification. Recently, there has been a shift to thinking of principals as instructional leaders. They are expected to be thoroughly aware of each classroom, the instructional styles of each teacher, and the learning outcomes of all students.

50. An appropriate district-level orientation activity for a group of new teachers is (Easy) (Skill 8.4)

   A. To discuss the philosophies of the highest performing schools in the district
   B. To introduce them to the senior staff who are shared between schools in the district
   C. To review the district's policy manual
   D. All of the above

Answer: C. To review the district's policy manual
Information about the district's policies is relevant at the district-level orientation. This is the most appropriate activity because it does not relate to a specific school and will be relevant to teachers from different schools.

51. In performance-based assessments the principal ties teachers' performance to: (Easy) (Skill 8.4)

   A. Student learning
   B. Parental feedback
   C. Administrative ratings
   D. Student surveys

Answer: A. Student learning
In performance-based assessments, the principal must tie teachers' performance to student learning.

52. An employee has been incompetent all year although you have followed all steps to help her. She has instituted a grievance against you for allegedly harassing her and claims that she is an excellent teacher as demonstrated by her work at other schools. You have documented her work and through the grapevine you learn that she was under personal stress but has recently resolved these issues. What should you do to decide her fate for the upcoming school year? (Average) (Skill 8.4)

   A. Terminate her
   B. Discuss the matter with another principal
   C. Rehire her because her performance was affected by personal problems that will no longer hinder her performance
   D. Evaluate her against the district's pre-selected criteria

Answer: D. Evaluate her against the district's pre-selected criteria
By using the districts pre-selected criteria the principal can remain objective in appraising staff. Additionally, because the personal information was obtained through the grapevine, it should be deemed unreliable and should not be used.

53. **A news exposé showed pictures of Monroe High School with missing ceiling tiles, broken toilets, and emergency doors that were jammed. The principal was supposedly unaware of these issues before the story aired. Which of the following is the most effective strategy for a principal to avoid falling into a similar embarrassing situation?**
(Rigorous) (Skill 9.1)

  A. Recognizing that the physical environment must be a top priority for the principal to oversee, perhaps by shifting his/her focus from overseeing instructional matters
  B. Encouraging the students and staff to report issues
  C. Using a checklist to review the physical environment, and if necessary, delegating the task to ensure that this check is performed routinely
  D. All of the above

Answer: C. Using a checklist to review the physical environment, and if necessary, delegating the task to ensure that this check is performed routinely
A principal or designee, such as an assistant principal, should be responsible for making routine, perhaps even daily, rounds on a campus in order to verify a checklist of items. Such items might include visiting restrooms to ensure that everything is working properly and that the school's facilities are clean and well-maintained.

54. **The opposite of an evacuation plan is a _____ plan.**
(Easy) (Skill 9.1)

  A. closed-campus
  B. panic-mode
  C. security-precaution
  D. lock-down

Answer: D. lock-down
The opposite of an evacuation plan would be a lock-down plan. A lock-down plan would consist of various rules and procedures for getting or keeping all students in secure locations such as their classrooms. The problem with a lock-down is that often communication suffers; this can be overcome if e-mail or other forms of communication can be used to update stakeholders during the lock-down.

55. Which of the following is an appropriate procedure for dealing with students who misbehave on a regular basis?
(Easy) (Skill 9.3)

A. Use modeling and coaching for students to learn appropriate behaviors
B. Trust that the students will behave and allow them freedom
C. Allow enough time so that while students transition from one class to another they can have down time
D. Use verbal private reprimands

Answer: A. Use modeling and coaching for students to learn appropriate behaviors
When dealing with students who misbehave on a regular basis, educators should follow the least restrictive and most developmentally appropriate course of action. This includes modeling the appropriate actions and coaching students to manage their behaviors. Do not expect results overnight. To reinforce positive behavioral changes, always praise students for good behavior.

DOMAIN IV COLLABORATING WITH KEY STAKEHOLDERS

56. Principals should seek to engage parents in the school's efforts. Which of the following is the greatest reason for involving parents?
(Easy) (Skill 10.1)

A. Because parents share a common desire for their children to do well
B. Because some parents had negative experiences when they were in school
C. Because some parents were star pupils
D. Because parents usually have little effect on a school's plans

Answer: A. Because parents share a common desire for their children to do well
All parents have deeply personal reasons to support the school's efforts; they want their children to do well in school.

57.   **Why must administrators ensure that outside agencies are involved in the operation of schools?**
    (Average) (Skill 10.1)

    A.   Students should be able to see how community organizations are interrelated
    B.   This helps students see that what they learn in school is connected to real life
    C.   Field trips and guest speakers help keep learning exciting
    D.   All of the above

Answer: D. All of the above
Outside agencies should be involved in the operation of schools because these organizations and individuals can enhance the learning experience. Learning outside the classroom or bringing different individuals into the school helps students see that what they learn in school is connected to real life. In addition, they provide a change of pace and students can realize that the community is interrelated and that each element is important.

58.   **Last year School Y was on the state's list of critically low-performing schools. No measurable gains were recorded during the second year and consequently, the school is on the list for two years in-a-row. Which of the following is the best strategy to support turn-around efforts?**
    (Rigorous) (Skill 10.1)

    A.   Involve the community to identify other schools that have been working to increase their performance.
    B.   Have a meeting with teachers and establish a strategic plan that focuses on increasing parental involvement in the school.
    C.   Secure advice from the state and district and work on the problem.
    D.   Create a committee of teachers, parents, students, and community members to obtain information and to develop a plan of action.

Answer: D. Create a committee of teachers, parents, students, and community members to obtain information and to develop a plan of action.
This approach involves a wide array of stakeholders. The team will help to create a plan of action that considers many perspectives and suggestions. In addition, it will facilitate buy-in for the work that will be necessary to implement the plan.

59. Your high school's drama academy recently won first-place honors at the State Thespian Festival. Which of these actions would BEST serve to engage the parents and community members who live near your school?
(Average) (Skill 10.1 B)

    A.   Schedule a free "open to the public" event at which students present their winning vignettes

    B.   Write an article for a nationally-recognized educational journal

    C.   Hold a news conference for the local newspaper, radio, and television organizations

    D.   Display the award on the activities board in front of the school

Answer: A. Schedule a free "open to the public" event at which students present their winning vignettes
By inviting parents and community members to attend the performance, students can showcase their work. This engages the community, advertises the program's success, and gives the community a real sample of what is going on in the school.

60. As the superintendent, you would like to propose that additional income be raised through an increase in property taxes. Why should a public relations campaign be utilized during this process?
(Average) (Skill 10.5 A)

    A.   To create a proposal that will highlight the benefits of the increase

    B.   To analyze and address the opinions, emotions, and interests of different community groups

    C.   To create a commercial that will be broadcast on the television station watched by most parents in the district

    D.   To collect data from the community that can be presented to the Board of Education

Answer: B. To analyze and address the opinions, emotions, and interests of the different community groups
A public relations campaign allows an organization to create targeted outreach efforts. Educational leaders must determine the audiences, forums, and time frames in which their message(s) will be delivered to the public. Different groups will have different opinions, emotions, and interests that need to be analyzed and addressed.

61. **Because schools are open systems and operate within a community environment, a school with an effective community relations program and a positive image may be more effective in:**
(Easy) (Skill 10.5 A)

    A. Obtaining federal grants to support school programs
    B. Securing support from the community to carry out projects
    C. Being selected to appear on television commercials
    D. Sending more of its graduates off to college

Answer: B. Securing support from the community to carry out projects
An effective school and community relations plan is important for the success of any school. Rather than simply disseminating information to community partners, relationships must be built to engage them. Such relationships increase support for the school and lead to increased satisfaction.

62. **Recommended practice suggests that which of the following should be involved in the decision-making process concerning school improvement?**
(Easy) (Skill 11.1)

    I. Teachers
    II. Community Partners
    III. Administrators
    IV. Parents and students

    A. I and III only
    B. II and III only
    C. I, III, and IV only
    D. I, II, III, and IV

Answer: D. I, II, III, and IV
Strategic planning for school improvement should include all stakeholders. All parties should have representation in the identification of improvement goals and the plan to attain them.

63. **When using site-based management, why should a principal involve a diverse group of stakeholders in the planning and decision-making processes? (Rigorous) (Skill 11.3)**

   A. The Civil Rights Act requires that diverse groups participate in all parts of school management
   B. It avoids conflict when choices are made because every person is represented by individuals on the committee
   C. A committee of diverse individuals cannot represent everyone; however, they are more likely to bring different perspectives compared to a non-diverse committee
   D. This guarantees that special-interest groups will not have grounds on which to bring legal action against the school

Answer: C. A committee of diverse individuals cannot represent everyone; however, they are more likely to bring different perspectives compared to a non-diverse committee
Schools are complex social systems involving a diverse range of students and teachers. Principals are successful when they can find ways to ensure that all students' sociological, linguistic, and cultural concerns are addressed.

64.   Ms. Martinez teaches World Geography at a high school where 60% of the students are Hispanic, 25% are African American, and 15% are European American. If she wants to benefit from the diversity of her students at the start the school year, which of the following would be the best project for her to assign?
(Rigorous) (Skill 11.4)

   A.   Give each student a map of the world on which to identify and color a list of countries; she would then display the maps.
   B.   Have each student locate his or her family's country(ies) or continent(s) of origin on a large world map. Then have students share their families' histories outside of and/or within the United States.
   C.   Have students work in homogeneous groups and compare the similarities and differences of their parents' families.
   D.   Give an overview of the semester's objectives; assign the first chapter of the textbook and have students work in groups to compare their answers to the questions at the end of the chapter.

Answer: B. Have each student locate his or her family's country(ies) or continent(s) of origin on a large world map. Then have students share their families' histories outside of and/or within the United States.
By having students locate their family's country(ies) or continent(s) of origin, the class would see the diverse parts of the world where students have ties. In addition, this accommodates those students who may not know exactly where their families originated outside of the United States. All students are able to participate because they have the opportunity to talk about their family history in the United States. Special considerations should be made for students who may not know their biological parents.

65.   When assessments incorporate cultural knowledge, history, experiences, and relevance of contextual knowledge, they are:
(Easy) (Skill 11.4)

   A.   Traditionally-focused
   B.   Knowledge-based
   C.   Culturally-responsive
   D.   All of the above

Answer: C. Culturally-responsive
Assessments must identify culturally-responsive teaching methods that incorporate cultural knowledge, history, experiences, and relevance of contextual knowledge.

66.   Keeping the campus safe and welcoming for all students is a _____ issue
        (Easy) (Skill 11.4)

        A.   cognitive
        B.   sociological
        C.   linguistic
        D.   cultural

Answer: B. sociological
Sociological concerns include keeping the school campus safe, secure, and welcoming for all
students.

67.   A principal learns that the district is requiring each school to have a coordinated
        technology plan. The directive requires that each week, each class uses the
        mobile technology lab to enhance learning. Identify the most cost-effective
        method to meet this need:
        (Rigorous) (Skill 12.3 A)

        A.   Analyzing the school schedule and appointing two team members who have a
                morning and an afternoon time slot to reallocate to this task
        B.   Selecting members of the student council who have already taken all their
                prerequisites and who have open slots in their schedules
        C.   Hiring a new staff member on a one year position approved by the teachers'
                union
        D.   Placing the laptops in an unused classroom and allowing teachers to bring their
                classes to the lab bi-weekly

**Answer. A. Analyzing the school schedule and appointing two team members who
have a morning and an afternoon time slot to reallocate to this task**
To be cost-effective when additional support is needed, before hiring new individuals, the
principal must assess how current staff is being used. He or she may find that the need can
be filled by reallocating team members.

68.   To reduce the chances of alienating the audience, a speaker must:
       (Average) (Skill 12.4)

       A.   Plan an in-depth report of facts and statistics to support his or her argument
       B.   Analyze his or her biases, emotions, and interests so they do not alter the message
       C.   Make an impassioned, emotional appeal
       D.   Solicit listener opinions after stating the objective

Answer: B. Analyze his or her biases, emotions, and interests so they do not alter the message
Analyzing his or her emotions, interests, and biases will allow a speaker to prepare a message that does not alienate audience members.

69.   Principal Brown has recently begun attending the local senior citizens' council meeting. In the short-term, the school can likely benefit from this relationship by:
       (Easy) (Skill 12.4)

       A.   Asking the group to fund a new addition to the school
       B.   Engaging members as reading volunteers
       C.   Having the organization lobby the city council on the school's behalf
       D.   None of the above

Answer: B. Engaging members as reading volunteers
The principal has only recently begun to support the community group; therefore, in the short-term, the school can likely engage group members to volunteer at the school.

70.   There are six phases of communication: ideating, encoding, transmitting, receiving, decoding, and acting. Which of the following includes one phase that involves the sender and one phase that involves the receiver?
       (Rigorous) (Skill 12.4 A)

       A.   Ideating and encoding
       B.   Receiving and decoding
       C.   Ideating and decoding
       D.   None of the above

Answer C. Ideating and decoding
Ideating is the development of the idea or message to be communicated. This is done by the sender. Decoding is the receiver's translation of the message. This is done by the receiver.

DOMAIN V ETHICS AND INTEGRITY

71. Why is a code of conduct an important document?
(Average) (Skill 13.1 B)

    A.   It identifies a committee that can be called upon if a situation arises and the code itself cannot provide adequate guidance.
    B.   To provide a litmus test for behaviors
    C.   It identifies pre-determined consequences for violators
    D.   All of the above

Answer: D. All of the above
A code of conduct provides a litmus test by which behaviors can be measured and addressed and it must include pre-determined steps for dealing with violators. If a situation arises and the code cannot provide adequate guidance, then the code-development committee must be reconvened to update the code.

72. A federal law that governs the disclosure of student education records is:
(Easy) (Skill 13.2)

    A.   HERPA
    B.   FERPA
    C.   FREPA
    D.   HEFPA

Answer: B. FERPA
One existing law that deals with confidentiality in the schools is FERPA. FERPA, the Family Educational Rights and Privacy Act, is a federal law that governs the disclosure of student education records.

73. Electronic files and computerized databases are kept secure by which of the following groups in the technology team?
(Average) (Skill 13.2)

    A.   Network
    B.   Hardware
    C.   Peripheral
    D.   CAI

Answer: A. Network
The network security team develops the plan to safeguard electronic files and computerized databases. They also monitor and handle threats and provide updates to the principal or appropriate administrator.

74. **To prepare students to be good citizens, the principal should do which of the following?**
(Rigorous) (Skill 13.3)

    A.   Encourage students to seek out role models who have achieved success in business
    B.   Foster an environment that emphasizes ethical principles, moral values, and civic participation
    C.   Encourage students to rethink cultural practices that are opposed to the norms and practices of the larger society
    D.   All of the above

Answer: B. Foster an environment that emphasizes ethical principles, moral values, and civic participation.
The principal should foster a school environment that helps each child to become a responsible citizen. Students should be encouraged to select role models based on their character, not their professions.

75. **A principal can serve as an ambassador by doing all of the following EXCEPT:**
(Average) (Skill 13.3)

    A.   Attending community events
    B.   Participating in meetings held by local groups
    C.   Joining important civic organizations
    D.   Serving as the school arbitrator for district-wide staff disputes

Answer: D. Serving as the school arbitrator for district-wide staff disputes
An educational leader must be an ambassador by attending community events, participating in meetings, and joining important organizations.

76. **Many people believe that a great educational system is necessary for a thriving society because:**
(Easy) (Skill 13.3)

    A.   It fuels economic growth
    B.   It fosters societal development
    C.   It focuses communities on preparing its children for productive citizenship
    D.   All of the above

Answer: D. All of the above
Education fuels economic growth, fosters societal development, and focuses communities on preparing its children for productive citizenship

77. **When an educational leader values each individual he or she will be:**
(Easy) (Skill 14.1)

A. Traditionally-focused
B. Knowledge-based
C. Culturally-responsive
D. Historically accurate

Answer: C. Culturally-responsive
To respect an individual, his or her culture must be respected and honored. This means the administrator must value each member of the learning community and his or her traditions, norms, values, history, and experiences.

78. **Which of the following is a strategy to foster a respectful and inclusive environment?**
(Easy) (Skill 14.1)

A. Creating a system of rewards and recognition
B. Developing effective teams
C. Establishing trust
D. All of the above

Answer. D. All of the above
Several strategies should be developed by administrators who want to foster this type of environment. They include:

- Utilizing strong communication skills
- Fostering collegiality, civility, and respect
- Creating a system of rewards and recognition
- Developing effective teams
- Establishing trust
- Managing stressful situations
- Supporting staff in times of change

79. In the organizational development approach, each person must feel that he or she has the autonomy to contribute something of value to the team. Autonomy comes from the key value of:
(Easy) (Skill 14.1)

A. Empowerment
B. Collaboration
C. Authenticity
D. Respect and inclusion

Answer. A. Empowerment
In the organizational development approach, individuals are empowered to help everyone in the community increase their autonomy to make the workplace and/or community satisfying and productive.

80. According to Galpin and Whittington, which of the following is NOT a ground rule that encourages authenticity and honesty?
(Average) (Skill 14.4 A)

A. Staying on the current topic
B. Participating in the discussion as often as possible
C. Agreeing to disagree if consensus can't be reached
D. Using active listening, including reading non-verbal language

Answer. B. Participating in the discussion as often as possible
In their 2009 article in the Journal of Leadership Education, Timothy Galpin and J. Lee Whittington suggest simple ground rules such as: Stay on topic; Do not over participate; Agree to disagree; Listen; Respect others' ideas; and Be brief.

81. According to the Society for Organizational Learning (SoL), making your thinking and reasoning more visible to others is called _____.
(Average) (Skill 14.4 A)

A. Reflection
B. Inquiry
C. Advocacy
D. None of the above

Answer. C. Advocacy
The Society for Organizational Learning (SoL) suggests:

- Becoming more aware of your own thinking and reasoning (Reflection);
- Making your thinking and reasoning more visible to others (Advocacy);
- Inquiring into others' thinking and reasoning (Inquiry).

82. **If a school has been identified as low-performing for the first year, the state may require that the School Improvement Plan include:**
    (Average) (Skill 15.1 A)

    A. Parent contracts for all students in the school
    B. Collective bargaining for all employees
    C. A plan for all administrators to engage in leadership-based professional development
    D. A take-over plan

Answer: C. A plan for all administrators to engage in leadership-based professional development
When a school fails to meet benchmarks established by the federal-government, state, or district, the School Improvement Plan (SIP) must include procedures for increasing the principal's ability to lead the school in its turn-around efforts.

83. **During times of crisis the principal can help the school stay on course by:**
    (Rigorous) (Skill 15.4)

    A. Talking about the crisis in the past tense so everyone remembers the situation is only temporary
    B. Keeping the vision and goals in the forefront of everyone's mind so the situation does not divert the school from its charted course
    C. Implementing an intensive long-term solution so that the team can work on the issue in segments
    D. Making sure that full energies are devoted toward the crisis so that it can be handled as quickly as possible

Answer: B. Keeping the vision and goals in the forefront of everyone's mind so the situation does not divert the school from its charted course
At all times, even during times of crises, an educational leader must keep the school's pre-determined plans at the forefront of everyone's minds. This is particularly the case when the team is focused on solving problems that seem unrelated to the vision and goals. These core planning tools can serve as roadmaps and can ensure that distractions do not divert the school from its charted course.

84. The _____ determines the longevity of the proposed solution and the probable recurrence of the same or similar difficulties.
(Average) (Skill 15.4 A)

   A.   quality of the problem-solving strategy
   B.   principal's ability to engage external stakeholders
   C.   level of communication with faculty members
   D.   ability to raise the necessary funds

Answer: A. quality of the problem-solving strategy
The quality of the problem-solving strategy determines the longevity of the proposed solution and the probable recurrence of the same or similar difficulties.

DOMAIN VI THE EDUCATIONAL SYSTEM

85. The U.S. Department of Education has recently updated the Elementary and Secondary Education Act (ESEA). In three years it will require the state to implement a new assessment that all students must master in order for them to graduate from high school. In the first month after the policy is announced, what is the best strategy to prepare parents for its implementation?
(Average) (Skill 16.1 A)

   A.   Post basic information on a bulletin board so parents can learn about the new policy
   B.   Call all parents so they are aware of the change and can make immediate preparations for their children who will have to take the assessment
   C.   Plan a pep rally for students in the neighborhood middle school so they are aware of the assessment they will need to take
   D.   All of the above

Answer: A. Post basic information on a bulletin board so parents can learn about the new policy
The change will take effect in three years; therefore, the best way to prepare parents is to post basic information so they can learn about the new policy. As the policy becomes more finalized, information should be posted and parents can be updated in other ways.

86. The school's boilers stopped working on Friday night and the school does not have a mass-calling system. Which method of communication is the most considerate, efficient, and cost-effective to inform parents that the school will be closed?
(Rigorous) (Skill 16.1 B)

    A.   Post a sign on the doors so parents know why the building is not open when they come to drop off the children
    B.   Send an email to all parents and ask that they respond confirming receipt. Then a plan can be created for parents who may not have received the information
    C.   Ask each teacher to call the homes of his/her first period students
    D.   None of the above

Answer: B. Send an email to all parents and ask that they respond confirming receipt. Then a plan can be created for parents who not have received the information
It may be found that a majority of the parents respond and only a few parents need to be contacted by other means. Email is typically faster, more effective, and more efficient compared to other methods of communication. It is likely that some parents may not check their email over the weekend. Requesting a confirmation email will allow a secondary plan to be created to inform those parents who do not respond to the email.

87. The acronym FAQ stands for:
(Easy) (Skill 16.1 B)

    A.   Faculty Area Questionnaire
    B.   Frequently Asked Questions
    C.   Faculty Assistance Questions
    D.   Frequently Assessed Questionnaire

Answer: B. Frequently Asked Questions
FAQ stands for Frequently Asked Questions.

88. **To facilitate discussion-oriented, non-threatening communication, administrators must do which of the following:**
   (Average) (Skill 16.1 B)

   A. Model appropriate behavior
   B. Allow other stakeholders to express themselves freely
   C. Explain that parents, teachers, and administrators are all working for the good of students and therefore, they should not disagree
   D. All of the above

Answer: A. Model appropriate behavior
To facilitate discussion-oriented, non-threatening communication, administrators must take the lead and model appropriate actions and speech. They must also practice strong facilitation skills to ensure that stakeholders communicate respectfully and appropriately. The administrator must help constituents realize that at times, people will have to agree to disagree.

89. **Administrators should network with other stakeholders for all of the following reasons EXCEPT _____?**
   (Easy) (Skill 16.2)

   A. To discuss challenges facing schools, teachers, and education in general
   B. To develop a sense of community
   C. To fulfill the necessary requirements for licensure renewal
   D. To find solutions to difficult problems

Answer: C. To fulfill the necessary requirements for licensure renewal
Administrators must network with other stakeholders. This allows school leaders to advance the cause of education. It also facilitates the integration of the school into the larger community and presents opportunities for problem solving to occur.

90. **Often, schools and communities interact for the following activities EXCEPT?**
   (Easy) (Skill 16.2)

   A. Blood drives
   B. Legal proceedings
   C. Meeting room use
   D. Elections

Answer: B. Legal proceedings
In some places, the community is one entity and the school is another and rarely do the two meet. Interactions may occur for blood drives and elections. In addition, because the gyms may be the biggest meeting rooms in the city or county, they can be utilized by the larger community.

91. When embracing diversity, educators must ensure that they neither protect students from criticism nor praise them because of their ethnicity or gender. Doing either action may result in which of the following outcomes?
(Easy) (Skill 16.3)

   A. Classmates may become anxious or resentful when dealing with the diverse students
   B. Parents will appreciate their child being singled out
   C. The child will be pleased to receive this attention
   D. Other teachers will follow this example

Answer: A. Classmates may become anxious or resentful when dealing with the diverse students

To create a school environment that embraces diversity, students should not be "protected" from criticism because of their ethnicity or gender. Likewise, acknowledge and praise all meritorious work without singling out particular students. Both actions can make all students hyper-aware of ethnic and gender differences and cause anxiety or resentment throughout a class or a school.

92. Of the following definitions, which best describes an evidence-based approach to academic planning?
(Rigorous) (Skill 17.1)

   A. It focuses on narrow skills and abilities
   B. It relies on assessment data to define the school's strengths and weaknesses
   C. It focuses on federal, state, and local standards
   D. It measures test performance related to specific, recently acquired information

Answer: B. It relies on assessment data to define the school's strengths and weaknesses

An evidence-based approach to academic planning relies on assessment data to define the school's strengths and weaknesses.

93. **Administrators must hold themselves to high standards. When they engage in negative actions such as fighting with parents, they are violating all of the following EXCEPT:**
(Easy) (Skill 17.2)

   A.   Ethics
   B.   Professionalism
   C.   Morals
   D.   Fiscal responsibility

Answer: D. Fiscal responsibility
Administrators must adhere to strict rules and regulations to maintain the highest degree of conduct and professionalism. It is imperative that today's educators have the highest regard for professionalism and behave as proper role models for teachers, parents, and students in and out of the school.

94. **Instructional design teams plan more effectively for instruction when they:**
(Average) (Skill 17.3)

   A.   Describe the role of the teacher and student
   B.   Rearrange the order of activities
   C.   Assess the outcomes of prior instruction
   D.   All of the above

Answer: C. Assess the outcomes of prior instruction
It is important to plan the content, materials, activities, and goals of each lesson. However, these steps will not make a difference if students are not able to demonstrate improvement in the skills being taught. The instructional design team must constantly adapt all aspects of the curriculum to what is actually happening in the classroom. Effective instruction occurs when educators assess the outcomes regularly and then make adjustments accordingly.

95. **Mr. Rogers describes his educational philosophy as eclectic, meaning that he uses many educational theories to guide his classroom practice. Why is this strategy the best approach for today's teachers?**
   (Rigorous) (Skill 17.3)

   A.   Today's classrooms are often too diverse for one theory to meet the needs of all students

   B.   If one theory is not effective educators must be able to draw upon other strategies

   C.   This allows the teacher to select from a variety of methods rather than being limited to one school of thought or practice

   D.   All of the above

Answer: D. All of the above
No one theory will work for every classroom; a good approach is for an educator to incorporate a range of learning theories in his/her practice. Still, under the guidance of any theory, good educators will differentiate their instructional practices to meet the needs of individual students' abilities and interests using various instructional practices.

CPSIA information can be obtained at www.ICGtesting.com
Printed in the USA
BVOW05s1116040214

343918BV00005B/140/P